UNCLE TOM COBLEY AND ALL
WIDECOMBE
IN-THE-MOOR

PHOTOGRAPHS AND MEMORIES OF DARTMOOR'S MOST FAMOUS PARISH

STEPHEN WOODS

HALSGROVE

First published in Great Britain in 2000

British Library Cataloguing-in-Publication Data
A CIP record for this title is available from the British Library

ISBN 1 84114 046 5

HALSGROVE
PUBLISHING, MEDIA AND DISTRIBUTION

Halsgrove House
Lower Moor Way
Tiverton, Devon EX16 6SS
Tel: 01884 243242
Fax: 01884 243325
website: http://www.halsgrove.com

Previous page: *Taken over the iron gate on the way home from school.
Left to right: Jean Nosworthy, Bernard Miners, Edna Brown, Joyce Miners, Tony Brown,
Dorothy Brown, Myra Miners, one of the two lady photographers,
Joan Miners, Phyllis Brown.* (Phyllis Pascoe née Brown)

Printed and bound in Great Britain by Bookcraft Ltd., Midsomer Norton

DEDICATION

This book is dedicated to the people of Widecombe-in-the-Moor past and present, especially to the members of Widecombe and District Local History Group.

May they be encouraged to go into print and safeguard knowledge so painstakingly researched and gained.

Ploughing on Southcombe.

Near Ponsworthy, 1898. The cottages on the right are known as The Splash. Bessie French (née Turner) now lives at No.2 and the end of the second building is the forge. (Robert Burnard)

FOREWORD

Over the last decade or so I have published two earlier books by Stephen Woods; his classic study *Dartmoor Stone* and *Widecombe-in-the-Moor*. The former work has established itself as one of the essential Dartmoor titles, a rare combination of information and beauty in a single volume.

Though the success of *Dartmoor Stone* was assured, neither Stephen nor I could envisage just how important his first book on Widecombe would be. There was no doubt about the value of its content – hundreds of images, most of them never before published, collected over many years, supported by a detailed text. But could such a book be successfully sold into a relatively small market?

As it turned out the book became a model for what has grown into the Halsgrove Community History Series, with over fifty titles now published and in production. These each contain many hundreds of photographs and detailed captions thus providing a 'living archive' for each community over the centuries. For his part in helping to establish the series I shall always be immensely grateful to Stephen.

Anyone who has a connection with Widecombe, and with Dartmoor in general, will, I know, enjoy the wonderful memories that Stephen's new book evokes.

Simon Butler
Halsgrove
January 2000

A photograph of the Vicarage Fête. Inscribed on the back are the words: 'In happy memory of Aug. 6 1931, Beatrice Chase.' (Julia Morley)

Emily and Ethel Kernick playing by the well in c.1890. Note the thatched roof of the ash house behind.
(Julia Morley)

The day Widecombe won the Daily Mail's *Village Sign Competition. Note the hedge behind, which was removed when the café on the green was built.* (Deborah Hannaford)

CONTENTS

ACKNOWLEDGEMENTS

It gives me great pleasure to acknowledge the help given so freely and by so many people. Those acknowledged by name in the previous volume are remembered once again, but those named below gave particular help for this second volume, some with both titles:

Norman Baldock, John Basire, Dorothy Baty, Tony Beard, Brenda Bovey, Kath Brewer, Philip Coaker, Eileen Exell, Bessie French, Elisabeth Greeves, Deborah Griffiths, Roger Grimley, Kit Hall, Winifred Harman, Judith Hervey, John Hooper, Brian and Suzanne Hutchins, Brian Le Messurier, Sylvester and Gladys Mann, Bernard Miners, Julia Morley, Kathleen Mortimore, Sylvia Needham, Michael Nosworthy, Phyllis Pascoe, John Pidgeon, Jack Prouse, Peter Rennells, Mary Rivers-Moore, Kate Van Der Kiste, Sir William Van Straubenzee, Geoff and Marjorie Weymouth, Freda Wilkinson, Ann Williams, Dorothy Williams.

Sunday School children, including the author at the right of the picture.

INTRODUCTION

This book is a continuation of the previous volume *Widecombe-in-the-Moor – A Pictorial History of a Dartmoor Village* and, as such, any reference made to previous writings on a given subject refer to that title.

At the time of writing I stated that I was not averse to criticism or disagreement and that I would welcome the chance of being advised of any new material. This book is the result of the response to that statement and has provided a welcome opportunity for me to expand upon and enhance earlier material, particularly with regards to farming and the agricultural community – a central part of Widecombe life.

I have long believed that there is such a wealth of information to be found about Widecombe Parish and its people that several volumes could be produced. Since the publication of *Widecombe-in-the-Moor*, Elizabeth Gawnes' painstaking research into Widecombe longhouses has been printed and I am extremely grateful to Jenny Sanders for collating her notes and taking care that they were not lost. My mother, Iris Woods, was an equally keen researcher, although little of her work went into print. The same can be said of Hermon French, and it was to prevent such effort being wasted and the knowledge being lost that publication of this second volume was sought. Reg Bellamy has also produced *Postbridge, The Heart of Dartmoor*, a wonderful companion volume to *Widecombe-in-the-Moor* and one which it is hoped this new effort will enhance rather than trespass upon. Along with *Postbridge* and *Widecombe*, Halsgrove has featured a number of other Dartmoor villages in their extensive Community History Series, among them *Manaton*, *Meavy* and *Lamerton*.

The area covered by this volume encompasses the civil parish of Widecombe and that section of land from Sherberton in the south to Two Bridges, and from there eastward to New House (the Warren House Inn), an area historically containing the ancient tenements for which Bishop Bronscombe ordained 'the sacraments in life and death' should belong to Widecombe.

I received many photographs which, though refusing to fit neatly into any plans for the book, were well worth preserving in published form for their incidental but fascinating detail. In a box of prints and negatives labelled 'Frederick French and Mary Caunter of Ollsbrim', for example, was a faded print of a baby in a pram (*above*). Whether or not this is Mary Caunter is debatable, but the style of transport alone was worth recording! Items that to some might not seem worth mentioning throw up the most fascinating glimpses of past ways of life, as did Phyllis and Ern Pascoe's wedding-present list, which described what they needed to set up home. The author remembers that he and his wife Val bought the latest twin-tub washing machine but Phyllis and Ern had no electricity and had more need for a candlestick and pots and pans.

A number of photographs taken in the 1800s by Lady Sylvia Sayer's grandfather, Robert Burnard (1848-1920), have been included and I am grateful to have been able to make use of this archive. I have also included a few of the memories recalled by Canon Hall, one such being about the beginning of National Insurance. Lloyd George's slogan was '9d. for 4d.' The parishioners had never paid tax because they had no money, all of it being tied up in their stock and farms, and when they heard about 9d. for 4d. they all called upon Canon Hall to help fill in forms. He came to one farmer and asked his age, only to be told that the farmer had no idea as to his years, date of birth or even his birthplace. 'Had he ever been baptised', the farmer was asked. He did not know. Canon Hall began to despair but then asked the man whether he could remember the great blizzard. 'Yes,' the farmer replied, 'I was a little child, 12 years old, rode a pony with a sack of meal over to Cockingford and just got back when it began.' The farmer got his 9d. for 4d.!

More photographs and facts arrived on other features of Widecombe life that had previously been covered but which served to create an even more detailed picture of local goings on. The village fair was one such subject. It is said that the schoolgirls used to sing 'Widecombe Fair, Nobody there' and it may be that the events leading up to the First World War were the foundation for this saying as they are an exact match for an entry made in the Southcombe diaries following the declaration of war in 1914.

In the previous volume the author told a humourous story about George Lark. The ink had hardly dried before Jack Prouse was in touch saying:

I can remember George Lark at Widecombe when I was a very small boy, and I was born in 1920. He was, in fact, 'a part of Widecombe'. It is said that in his youth he was a very good dancer. I recall him as someone who worked at odd jobs for various farmers.

The wedding day of Phyllis Brown and Ern Pascoe, 8 June 1946, and receipts for the necessaries of the wedding and setting up home. Left to right, main picture: Helena Pascoe, Herbert 'Pickles' Pascoe, Ern Pascoe, Phyllis Pascoe, Jack Brown, Edna Brown, 'Mother' Brown. (Phyllis Pascoe)

And this is how he is recorded in the Southcombe Diaries:

He used to sharpen hand saws in the vice in the forge. Somewhere along the line there was a connection with my grandfather, Richard Kernick, who owned the forge, and I seem to recall that someone once told me that my grandfather had purchased the forge from George Lark's family but of that I am not certain. However, I do know that for many years George lived behind the bellows in the forge and that my grandfather insisted that he be allowed to stay there in spite of the many complaints from the blacksmith who was often hindered by having to move away from the fire whilst George fried his meal! I have often seen at two a.m., after the end of a dance at the Parish (Church) Hall, the village lit up by the reflection of the smithy fire where George was keeping warm! He burnt more coal at night than the blacksmith used by day!

George had peculiar ways – who hasn't? But everyone knew him and did not worry about them. He was always very suspicious that someone was trying to poison him and if anyone strange was in the village George would think they were after him and he would hide until they had gone. The only relation he had, so far as I know, was a nephew, Harry Lark, who was either the blacksmith or ran the public house at Denbury...

It must have been one day in about 1936 or '37 that he was taken ill and he died behind the bellows. I would think that a doctor must have attended as I do not recall any inquest. He was in fact the first dead person that I had ever seen. I with three others carried him on a mattress from the forge up into the Parish Hall. My aunt, Miss Mary Kernick, a very religious and dedicated person who had been nursing all her life, was on holiday at the time and was with him during his last hours. She insisted on washing him... after his death, saying George Lark was not going to enter the Kingdom of Heaven other than in a clean condition. My mother and two or three other ladies organised a collection around the parish to cover the cost of the funeral. No doubt my uncle, Louis Prouse, the undertaker, and the other necessary factors kept their prices as low as possible, and there was a balance from the collection sufficient to purchase and erect a headstone to his grave. He was buried in Widecombe churchyard on the site opposite the narrow path leading to Sentry (Sanctuary) Field and the graves of Beatrice Chase (O.K. Parr) and her mother. As far as I know the headstone is still there.

It will be seen here and throughout the book that correspondence is quoted verbatim and this is central to the book's aim, for the history is the result of talking to people and it is their knowledge that is transcribed here.

Stephen H. Woods

Lily Hambley (front centre left) and Iris Woods (front centre right) with their great- and great-great-grandchildren. Those present include Martin Morley (back centre), Philip Nicol (back right) and Diana Nicol holding Katherine (front right).
(Julia Morley)

✿ Jubilee ❧ Celebrations

Left: *Tree planting, Silver Jubilee, 6 May 1935. Left to right: Revd Wood, Billy Bray, Albany Brown, Mr King, Miss Penngaskell, Revd L.J. McCrea.* (Julia Morley)

Below, main picture: *Races on the green before all the village enjoyed a tea and the children each received a commemorative mug.*
Inset: *Green Café, Silver Jubilee, 1935.* (Julia Morley)

Above: *Mr Penn, Mr King and Miss Penngaskell of Scobitor hard at work.*

Left: *Silver Jubilee, 1977, for Queen Elizabeth II. Helping with the tree planting from left to right are: Simon 'Ned' Northmore, Brian Hutchins, John 'Jack' Brown, Ern Pascoe.* (Julia Morley)

Right: *The honoured tree planters had all been alive for Queen Victoria's Golden Jubilee. Left to right: Miss Norman, Mrs John Brown, Mr John Brown, Mrs Iris Woods, Mrs Lily Hambley, Miss May Harvey.* (Julia Morley)

Leusdon Jubilee ❦ Stone 1977 ❦

Top left: *What was to become the 1977 Leusdon Jubilee Stone lying in the hedge at Primms Hill.*

Top right: *Raising the stone, clockwise from top left: David French, Jess Wilkinson, Roy Hill, Michael Nosworthy, Terry French.*

Above left: *Veronica 'Ronnie' Cave Penny inspecting the stone.*

Above: *Simon Partridge (left) and Miles Fursdon (right) directing the loading of the stone for transportation.*

Left: *The Leusdon Jubilee Stone finally in place.*

(All photographs Marjorie and Geoff Weymouth)

Jim Smith, moorman of Hexworthy, 1941. (Sylvia Needham)

Widecombe ❧ Fair ❧

Clockwise from top: *Widecombe Fair, c.1905/10; again in the same period* (both May Hambley)*; 1931, behind the Old Inn* (Sylvia Needham)*; the festivities in 1990; and c.1940* (Hermon French Collection)*.

Top: *Venton Farm with Beatrice Cottage attached.*
Above, main picture and inset: *Photographs by Chapman & Son of the interior of Olive Katharine Parr's cottage and of Venton Chapel.* (Iris Woods)

Chapter 1: Widecombe Folk

❧ Our Lady of the Moor ❧

The following intriguing note appears in the Southcombe Diaries on 17 March 1919: 'Marion to the church to White Knight's Wedding'. The identity of the White Knight was to remain a mystery to me until Mr W. A. Saxton, Reader in the Moorland Team Ministry, kindly looked up the reference and wrote back:

White Knights is an easy one; William Joseph Adams RN, bachelor of full age, married, by licence, Dorothy Sanders of Manor Cottage, daughter of Fredk Sanders, Clerk. The witnesses were Olive Katharine Parr and Albert Edgar Adams, a brother, perhaps? Adams was from HMS Onyx, *in Torquay.*

Mr Saxton continued: 'I was a white knight in the unit mentioned in the brass memorial plaque (in the church) of the Radcliffe's – the 7th Battalion of the KRRC.'

The White Knights' Crusade was founded by Olive Katharine Parr (the authoress Beatrice Chase) during the First World War, with the aim of encouraging servicemen to be pure and noble. A book was kept in which their names were inscribed, and prayers were said in the chapel on their behalf. A revival during the Second World War received little attention.

It may be thought by some that Beatrice Chase affected a style of writing intended only for publication, but the wartime letters below reveal much about her lifestyle and give readers a chance to judge for themselves. The 'Wounded Warrior' was one Captain McGibbon, a Canadian doctor wounded during the 1914-18 conflict and who stayed at The Little Home of Rest, St Michael's, Venton, which Katharine (*above*) made available for those recuperating from their injuries.

Above: *Olive Katharine Parr's cottage door.*

Right: *The first of her letters to Captain McGibbon.*

17

Top: *Venton Cottages, postmarked 1946.* (Julia Morley)

Above left: *A photograph of Olive Katharine Parr by Chapman & Son.* (Ena Prowse)

Above: *Arthur Hern hedging at the top of Rugglestone Hill. With his mother and sister, Annie, Arthur farmed Lower Venton Farm.* (Beatrice Chase, 1931)

Left: *Olive Katharine Parr at her 'wishing well' with Tweed Dog.*

❧ Letters to a ❦ 'Wounded Warrior'

Letter 1 (June 24):

June 24.

Dear "Wounded Warrior"
Mr Oxenham is going to put me in prison for infringmenet
of copyright.

Isnt it sport?
MANY thanks for your
cheeky telegram.I dont THINK one shaft is lost on me.I grasp
the "Olive Katharine Parr"without the barmaid "Miss" to spoil it.
I hate "Miss" when I send envelopes addressed to myself for some
one to write in,I generally put my name with no prefix.And then
the polite people carefully spoil it by adding the Miss on top.

we are much tickled at the "All the famly".

Pray,sir,how much family have you got.?

I had another wire today--almost as cheeky as yours,from poor
Mr Oxenham.Every day we arrange to meet and every day the Lord
sends floods of rain.Today,Mr O wired "No luck.Am going to prison.
Jonah'".

Henceforth he wil be called Jonah.He signed one
letter to me in which he told a more than usualy stupendous
falsehood "george Washington".

Isnt George Washington the patron of all Yankees ?
I hope you dont feel that at all personal?
Now having got a bit of my own back by calling YOU a
Yankee,I will conclude and begin writing dreary and respectable
letters to booksellers.

Aquinate got a run in again this morning,drat him.He was writing to
a strange bookseller and saying "I want someone to push the book" and
with his usual low cunning he altered one letter and
said "I want someone to pish the book".Do you see the difference.?
In english(not in Yankee lingo)the exclamation "Pish" is one of
supreme contempt.

Ship dog has vanished since your departure.
Turk dog I have ordered to be shut up for a week.His master has
just been here bare headed and tremulous with apology.Turk Dog
has been here days and days(thanks to your injudicious feeding)
and is becoming a Public Curse.He has torn down Mrs Palmer's
washing line,buried the clothes in the garden bed,and torn one of
Mr Blue Jacket's flannels.He has so ruined a bolster cover, a sheet,
and other things that they have all got to be washed again.

I shd like to make you come out and wash them,sir.And if you
have any more idle ours hanging around---look out for yourself !

We are YEARNING to know more of Mrs McGibbon.

just in from Plymouth.Alas and alas !

We is to be here about on at,so if you come put to fetch
washing and to do MrsPalmer's washing for her,you will or may
see him.

Yours gratefully
B C

Turk is to be locked up day and night for a week.Yah !

did I tell you that
something rim is on at Land's end ?Palmer and seven other veteran
pensioners is guarding the wireless there.They sleep on the floor
all day and all eight are on duty every night and all night,with
a magistrate.I suppose its German submarines having a try.
That wireless there carries 3,000 miles and took the Lusitania's
message.

Friday. No news from you today!

Letter 2 (July 2):

July 2.

Dear Wounded Warrior,
You are a kind and a "clever pet".
Its THg feast today--the day I first entered Widecombe 13 years
ag.And I have been out into the lily bed to see if the
lilies are open enough and they arent.
And behold,LOVELY sweet peas--perfect,the three colours I most
love.And the other peas,the first we have had.

I am over joyed.you are kind beyond words.
I am going to do the altar vases immediately after lunch.
Blessings on you.Thine,

OKP

Letter 3 (July 2):

Venton House,
Widecombe-in-the-moor
Nr Ashburton
Devonshire July 2

My dear Captain, I want you to be kind enough to wait on a bit
longer in Ashburton till we see how I go on!
It rather seems that I have had or am having the same as
Mrs Mc Gibbon!
I have been feeling seedy for several days, on Monday I
had a bad backache, later spots came out on one elbow, a quantity of
them very irritable indeed. I did not think much about these
symptoms as I fancied I might have got some midges up my
sleeve, but yesterday I had a Temperature.
It is down today, so far below normal, but it is early yet in the
afternoon.
It is most mysterious as I have no other symptoms and feel much
better today in myself.
But my trouble is whether it is right to the ladies who
follow to let you both return.
Of course typhoid is not infectious, but this rash
seems so odd. I have never had anything like it in my life before,
it has died down, only lasting two days, and has not so far come
anywhere else.
I have written to tell Dr Savery.
But have not sent for him so far as I am better.

I shall be bitterly disappointed if you dnt come out again,
but I am sure you will see my point as to whether it is fair on
these poor ladies who come down in poor health, much run down,
as there would seem to be something catching

Olive is all right, but she does nothing with St Michael's
affairs, and I have all the time seem to the washing before sending
to the laundry and such like.

So please wait a little longer and let us see how things go.
I am not feeling up to the mark at all, though better than I
have been.

With love to both
Yours very sincerely
Katharine Parr

Letter 4 (July 23):

July 23

My dear Captain,
I wonder so much how your dear wife is
getting on. We are having such troubles with our letters here that
an inquiry is being made by an influential person in the London
G. P. O. so I dont know if you have written and we have not had
it.

If you know of any Officer this little place would benefit
we will do our utmost for him and His belongings.
The cottage will he at liberty on August 26th.
Three ladies have been before often will be in it till then,
with every good wish to you both.
Yours very sincerely
Katharine Parr.

Dear Wounded Warrior,
I was going to write to you today as ever is;and having found
Mother's sheet,I am gathering at the end of it.

You are a very privileged person to have a letter from The
Rainbow Maker and ME on one sheet.
I hope you are quite well.I hope Mrs Mc Gibbon is quite well.
We shd love to hear from you,if only a p.c.to say how things
are going.I THINK its just about now
she will be sailing back.I am therefore thinking of you both
more than usual every day.My whole sympathy is with you
both.Its beyond words.

Why I was going to write to you is because your lovely photographs
returned from the framer's on Friday and they are absolutely
beautiful--real works of art.They are framed in dark brown
if you know what brown is.The mounts are dull olive green,if you
know what olive green is.Being a man,I suppose you dont.

And I have hung them one above the other in the dining room
window above the Devon ware china,against my black
oak writing table.They show from every point there,and give
such an air of richness to the room.And as I sit there or in the
arm chair,I can see them constantly.You cant have hit on a thing
to give me greater and more constant joy.

Mr Oxenham is dedicating his next book to Olive Katharine Parr.
Its called "The Flower of the Lust" and appears in the autumn.

I do think its so kind of him.The Window is doing very well.
I am very much satisfied with the first three weeks of the sales.

I hope you liked it when you read it all.
Some people much prefer it to the HEART,others dont.so there you
are.Some say there is too much of me in it.Others say its too
lightful because I am in it at last.No accounting for tastes.
But any way,there is a book to suit each class.And next time,
I shall give them a Cornish story,a love story,all story.
This will be a complete change .We shall see how they like
that.

One shop in Torquay has a window beautifully done with it.
A cardboard "cut out"shaped like a window,with the book
standing in it,lots of copies,decorated with sprays of heather.
And "Interesting new Dartmoor book by Beatrice Chase"under it.

The reviews are fine.The Western Daily Mercu has reviewed it and
Answered Prayers together.It says whether Miss Chase is Miss Parr or
Miss Parr is Miss Chase,doesnt matter as long as they produce such
books as these.I say it matters to me,if not to them ! They say
no one not utterly scared fibred od scoff at Answered Prayers.
And it says how intensely real the people are in the Dartmoor Window
so "unlike the papier mache peasants of the town bred novelist"
I think papier mache peasant is one of the happiest terms I ever
heard.But its all very consoling to me because of the bold way
in which I have invaded Eden Phillpotts's country.

Then the next literary excitement is that Mr Oxenham have dramatis
my book "The Little Cardinal".He threw it into some of for me,
gave me general instructions about play writing
and went back to London leaving me to write the whole.
A Play is all dialogue,you see.,no description whatever.
Its frightfully interesting and utterly new stye of writing to
me.But its fascinating beyond words.Much more fascinating than
book writing.Its all so alive.You see your people.
Aquinate and I did it in five days.
Mr Oxenham suggested Forbes Robertson as THE man to play the
Cardinal.He says he isnt going to produce another play,ever,
or ever act again in England and only once again in the States.
However he is reading it now.we shall see.Any way I hope it will
be played in London for Xmas.And then I shall begin to swim in
gold.what people make byplays is something wicked.
Tiger is well and sweeter than ever.The Tweed Dog is well.
Please write soon.With much sympathy, OK Parr. How's the hand?

The sower, James Beard (the postman), who farmed Higher Bonehill Farm. (Beatrice Chase, 1931)

Cutting vags. (Beatrice Chase, 1931)

George Nosworthy harnessing the plough. (Beatrice Chase 1931)

George Nosworthy ploughing the ley. (Beatrice Chase 1931)

Above left: *Margaret Harris (née Nosworthy) at Higher Venton Farm where her father, George, farmed before moving to Wooder Farm.*
Above right: *Getting in the hay.* (Beatrice Chase 1931)

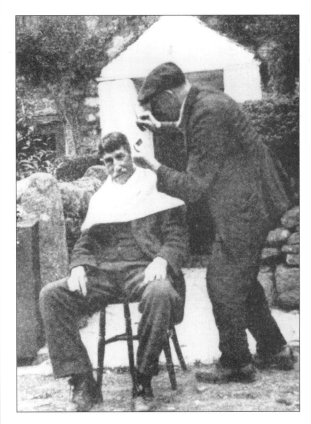

Above left: *Hair cutting.* (Beatrice Chase 1931)
Above right: *Lily Hambley (née Kernick).* (May Hambley)

❧ The Mysterious Lady Drake ❦

Agreat many years before Beatrice Chase became an eccentric, locally renowned character, there was another, even more fearsome, lady living in the village. The author's interest was aroused by a single cryptic line among his mother's notes: 'Stories abound in the village about Lady Drake'. Unfortunately, not a single story was forthcoming on the subject until Deborah Hannaford sent a handwritten article, penned nearly 50 years ago, bearing the attached note: 'For Deb – Lady Drake'. Its author was Lady Sylvia Sayer who gave permission for it to be quoted:

Was 'Lady Drake' of Widecombe really a granddaughter of King George IV? No one will ever know now. But about 100 years ago the truth might have been discovered in a lonely Dartmoor vicarage, where her uncle, the Reverend James Mason, occasionally dropped a hint or two over his excellent port as to his own and his sister's illustrious but illegitimate parentage. That sister, deserted by her husband, had died, leaving the little Caroline in James Mason's care – if care it could be called; for Parson Mason, exiled from Court to the wilds of Widecombe, was an embittered man who drank hard and kept strange company.

A gentleman by the name of Drake came to the Vicarage on business, and stayed to marry Caroline. Soon afterwards, her uncle died, leaving her his money and much valuable furniture and plate; Caroline then bought Widecombe Manor, and moved into the house with her husband, dogs and horses (she kept a dozen horses, and the village said they were fed on beer). From that time she insisted on being called 'Lady' Drake, and the domineering element in her character took the upper hand. Her husband bowed before it and allowed himself to be bullied and ruled. As Caroline resented his subservience and despised him for it,

Portrait of Reverend James Holman Mason. (Keith Fox)

they were not a happy pair. Mr Drake not unnaturally took to drink, and his life became more miserable than ever.

Caroline would send him to do the shopping chores in Ashburton in a small trap used for fetching coal, with a list of her requirements scribbled on a scrap of paper. One of these lists read: 'Kidney beans and cucumbers; tea, and green paint with driers; brushes and putty; sweets; and a frock-body for myself; a milk-pan, 14 inches; side combe, 3s.6d.; ostler's boy and fish; lavender; painkiller; wine, salad oil, harness paste and rice; also ribs of beef, grate for blue bedroom, india rubber; rabbits, grind scissors, cheese, inn and ostler.'

At last the downtrodden husband drank himself to death, and when friends commiserated with his widow she sharply replied 'Yes, he's dead. He might have done worse; he might have lived.' And she sent him to his coffin with a pigcloth for a winding sheet.

The last years of her own life were a nightmare time at the Manor. The house became filthy, swarming with dogs and cats; nothing could be done without 'her ladyship's' orders, and the servants never knew when to serve a meal or when they might go to bed, for their mistress often sat up by the fire all night. She died quite suddenly, self-willed and autocratic to the end. No blood-relations could be traced, and she left no will. One room in the house had been kept padlocked and she had kept the key attached to her garter: after her death her trustees found the room filled with a jumbled mass of furniture, crested silver, guineas and bank notes, thickly blanketed with dirt and cobwebs. There were letters too, but these were all destroyed.

'Lady' Drake was said to have resembled her reputed royal grandfather, but no portrait of her remains to give its evidence now; whatever the secret of her ancestry may have been, it died with her and can never now be solved.

The Dymond Diaries also give one a good insight into Lady Drake's character:

July 6th 1871

We had such a funny scene at dinner-time; soon after we had begun Mrs or rather Madame Drake appeared to pay her first call – rather awkward as she had to come straight into the hall where we were all seated up. However, we console ourselves with thinking that the lady of the Manor is accustomed to pretty many queer scenes in strange places and was probably more anxious to see Mrs Wills' 'young pegs' for which she affectionately enquired than to sit up and talk proper to us.

July 25th

After dinner the Mother and Cassie accompanied by Townsend drove over to the Manor House to return Mrs Drake's call – 'Madame' was found 'en desha- bille' being in the midst of preparations for visitors expected today. Of Mr Drake the less that is said the better. We saw enough of him to make us glad to accept Mrs Drake's proposal that we should look at her flowers – and were not sorry when the green gate closed behind us.

21st July 1884

The Father and Mother then went to see Mrs Drake, always a very pitiable object, she was now far worse than they had seen her – asleep in the kitchen – where the farm man ate his dinner, and the maid washed the clothes – her grey hair uncovered by cap or bonnet – she stared at us with filmy blind eyes – tho' when told who her visitors were she seemed to understand and with great difficulty went into the parlour, but she heard nothing that was said to her and looked so wretched and ill that they thought she could not live long and they came away saddened by the miserable scene, and by the thought that there was no way of helping her.

Caroline Mason Drake died on 14 March 1885, two years after her husband's death in 1883. At the time she owned Wooder House along with 62 acres of land, and Coombe plus 93 acres (tenanted by Robert Hern). Also in her possession were the following: 'a plot of pasture and waste ground known as part of Northall, 21 acres' (tenanted by William Nosworthy); 'a plot of pasture and waste ground known as part of Northall' (covering four acres and tenanted by S. Hern); and 'a plot of pasture tillage and waste land known as Lower Bartons of 18 acres' (tenanted by D. Follett). These last three pieces of land are, as far as is known, all that was left of the original North Hall (later known as Widecombe Town Manor).

Lady Drake also left behind her a cottage tenanted by S. Warren), a cottage in ruins and a blacksmith's shop tenanted by R. Kernick. There is some evidence that she owned the mill which might be the unnamed cottage in the tenancy of John Warren.

She left no will and her heir, Albert Brodrick, who was in considerable debt, had great difficulty in claiming the estate. Among the many docu- ments prepared to help Albert Brodrick establish his claim is one drafted by his mother, Matilda Salter Brodrick, an 85-year-old widow who set down her family tree and that of her husband as far as she could remember it. 'Point 30' noted that there was:

... issue of the said marriage of the said James Brodrick with the said Sarah Hooper Brodrick formerly Sarah Hooper Mason one child only namely Caroline Mason Brodrick who afterwards intermarried with the late Thomas Edward Drake and has recently died.

As the reader can see, there is no hint of any Royal scandal here – and there we must leave the mysterious Lady Drake.

❧ Sally and Thomas Satterley ❧

According to William Crossing, 'squatting' was still practiced in the early 1800s. If a house could be erected and a piece of land enclosed in a single day between sunrise and sunset, the builder could, it was said, claim it as his own. The last instance of such an event occurred in c.1835 when a small house, now known as Jolly Lane Cot, was built by Thomas Satterley at the side of the road leading down to Huccaby Bridge on the West Dart.

Everything was in readiness and the farmers of the neighbourhood safely departed to Ashburton Fair – as holders of the ancient tenements they had rights on the forest and would, it was feared, have prevented the Satterleys' plans. Everyone cheerily lent assistance and even before the walls at one end of the house were up, the laying of the thatch had begun at the other. By evening all was done, the 'squatters' were in possession and, as the story goes, a peat fire was burning on the hearth.

When the farmers returned from Ashburton, they did not take action, perhaps because Thomas had built the cottage to house his aged parents or perhaps because of the site he had chosen; the dwelling opposite is known as 'The Bearas', meaning 'not suitable for crops'.

Thomas Satterley's parents lived out their lives in the humble cottage, a fact which is recorded in the Widecombe Burial Register in 1845: 'Jane Satterley Hexworthy April 6th 74, John Satterley Hexworthy May 11th 75.'

In 1841, in Lydford Parish Church, Thomas was married to Sally Hannaford of Peat Cot, near the Whiteworks Mine, Princetown, and after his parents died, he moved with her to his parents' home.

A character in her own right, Sally was employed in the mine at Eylesbarrow. She drove pack horses, could cut peat, mow with a scythe, nail a shoe to a horse's hoof as well as a blacksmith and fish for salmon with a spear. She was at births and most deaths in the neighbourhood and would ride off to them at any hour of the day or night. It was her proud boast that 'her never lost one' in childbirth. One husband got so drunk when he was sent off for bread that he was three days returning.

Sally laid out the dead and was an important figure at local funerals. Bearers walked seven or eight miles to Widecombe churchyard and stopped at Coffin Stone on Dartmeet Hill for a drink. Sally generally walked in front, sometimes singing. She died in 1901 at the age of 87 and is buried in Widecombe churchyard.

Jolly Lane Cot, c.1885, and (above) Sarah Satterley, aged about 80, known to all as Sally.

Two Bridges and the Saracen Head Hotel where Thomas Satterley was ostler. (Frith's Series, Iris Woods)

❧ Charlotte Rosamund Larpent ❧

There appears to be no reason why Charlotte Larpent came to be interested in the people of Leusdon and the surrounding area – then the lower part of Widecombe parish and known to this day as Lower Town. Charlotte was a wealthy widow and became the benefactress of the Leusdon people, who must have come to believe wholeheartedly in her good works.

It was in 1829 that Charlotte Rosamund Arnold of Halstead Place, Kent, married Francis Seymour Larpent, becoming his second wife. He was involved in the inquiry into the 'Shocking Massacre at Princetown Prison' and, because of this, his name was probably known to many more than was that of his wife during their marriage.

The prison's Agent (Governor), Captain Shortland, believed that he had discovered a plot among a group of prisoners to escape and promptly sounded the alarm. The guards formed up in lines to be faced by an outpouring of POWs eager to see what was going on. In the confusion the order was given to fire and five Americans fell dead, two others died later and many more were wounded.

The Government ordered an immediate inquiry which was carried out by two men, Francis Seymour Larpent, an English advocate, and an American, Charles King. Having interviewed those involved, the two men reached the conclusion that 'no malice was involved' and reported back to the Government, who accepted their findings and agreed to pay compensation, all within a period of 24 days. Imagine how long it would take today!

A photograph by Chapman & Son of Princetown Prison (Iris Woods) *and* (inset) *a plan of the prison and barracks.* (Elisabeth Stanbrook)

Dartmoor convicts on their way to work.

Plymouth Road, Princetown, from Valentine's series, 1904. (Elisabeth Stanbrook)
Inset: *Dartmoor Convict Prison boundary stone.*

Aerial view of Leusdon School and schoolhouse, with Mrs Larpent's residence and (below) the first school and schoolhouse.

F. S. Larpent died in 1845, leaving Charlotte to outlive him by over 30 years. It was during this period, when she made frequent visits to Leusdon from her home in Torquay, that the village people caught and held her attention. She became interested firstly in the education of the children and, later, in the villagers' spiritual wellbeing.

It was probably a period of inclement weather that made her aware of the plight of the local children, who, if they were to learn to read and write, had to walk or ride to Widecombe every day. Charlotte must have acquired some of her husband's ability as an advocate for she was able to persuade one person after another to donate money and support her plans.

In 1855, Reverend Thomas Fry, Lord of Spitchwick Manor, gave a piece of land of approximately one acre to the vicar and church-wardens of Widecombe as a site on which to build a charity school. The area is now known as Leusdon Green or The Triangle. Although the land was not enclosed, it was surrounded by the tracks from Poundsgate, Lower Town and Ponsworthy which left a triangle of grass between them. On this land and just above the well (whose dilapidated ruins can still be seen) Charlotte Larpent built the schoolhouse at her own expense, together with a separate cottage for the teacher where she retained one or two rooms for herself to be used on her visits.

The first teachers, Mr Dobell (1855) and Thomas Vesey (1857) were male, which is interesting bearing in mind the fact that country charity schools were usually referred to as dame schools. Thomas Vesey was followed by a series of lady teachers, including Caroline Mogridge (1861), Anne Mare (1868), Susan Tucker (1872) and Mary Langfield (1875).

It would seem that Charlotte gave full financial assistance to the school as well as practical help with lessons, hearing the children read and recite and helping to teach them hymns and psalms. One of Her Majesty's Inspectors wrote: '[the school] stands through the Golden Wand of a benevolent lady, like an oasis in the desert.' However, feedback from the HMI reports was not always good as the school was so strongly influenced by the local clergy that their teachings of the Liturgy, Catechism, Collects and Scripture threatened that of the 'three Rs'.

As the years passed, Charlotte became more and more involved in the school and added further rooms to the teacher's house until it became a substantial residence, although admittedly it has something of a rabbit-warren appearance as each new room was added in a straight line to the last. It also had good gardens, a greenhouse, a coach house and a stable. The 1871 Census Returns list the following inhabitants: Charlotte Larpent, Widow lady, 77; Jane H. Saxby, boarder, Lady's companion, 32; Anne Mare, Lodger, School Mistress, 23; Louisa Mare, Assistant Mistress, 20.' There was also a groom/gardener, his wife (who was the cook) and a house parlour maid.

Having got the school at Leusdon up and running, Charlotte Larpent set about building a church, a residence for the vicar, Revd Wilkinson (followed by Revd Jackson) and a dwelling for his man, Richard Turner from Corndonford Farm.

To build the church, Charlotte needed the permission and support of the vicar and church-wardens, who had glebe lands in the area, of which she purchased 12 acres, so that they could be given 'freehold and unemcumbered,' at the same time promising accom-modation for the vicar and his man. Consent also had to be sought from the Bishop of Exeter, the fiery Henry Phillpotts (known as Henry of Exeter) whose speeches in the House of Lords often upset the Government. Charlotte not only got his consent, however, but Henry Phillpotts also presented the new church with its font.

Building began in 1862 and the church was dedicated the following year. On 1 March 1864 the southern part of the parish was formed into a

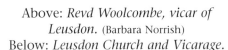

district chapelry called Leusdon and so became a parish in its own right. The civil parish was to remain the same.

Charlotte kept her promise and built the vicar's residence and a house for his man which may have been joined together to form the present Vicarage. In 1870 the National School came into being under the auspices of the vicar and churchwardens of Leusdon, and in 1872 Char-lotte built a house for the school's mistress next to the schoolroom and near her orig-inal premises. She died on 28 April 1879 and by her will left her house, garden and appur-tenances to a Mrs Ellerman who then claimed the school-house and adjoining building.

The Attorney General had to be called in by the charity commissioners on whose land all the residences and school buildings had been erected. It was seen by all that Charlotte Larpent had generously financed all of the good works for the ben-efit of others. It was deemed to be in the spirit of such events that there be a mutual agreement between the parties

Above: *Revd Woolcombe, vicar of Leusdon.* (Barbara Norrish)
Below: *Leusdon Church and Vicarage.*

that the Trustees convey to Mrs Ellerman the house, flower garden and stable, and she to them the school buildings, vegetable garden and other ground from the original conveyance of 1855.

When Leusdon School was finally closed, the land and buildings were returned to Spitchwick Manor – according to what must have been part of the original agreement. Roy Hill purchased the schoolhouse and schoolroom from where he runs a business as an undertaker and carpenter.

No connection has been found between Charlotte Rosamund Arnold of Kent and the Arnolds, or Arnells, of Uppacot and Sweaton. There is, however, a little twist in the tale of the name Larpent. At the other end of the parish a property at Wooder was owned by Baron de Hochepied (who called the building the South Devon County Hotel). At the same time his six sisters, the Misses

Above: An early photograph of the interior of Leusdon Church, taken before the pews were removed.
Below: Building the memorial to Charlotte Larpent. Left to right: Mr Cleave, George Avery, Richard Turner, ?.
(both Bessie French)

de Hochepied, also bought a property at Wooder, where Baron de Hochepied lived until his death in 1903 (after the hotel business had gone bankrupt).

John Larpent married twice; he had a son, Francis Seymour, by his first wife, and two sons by his second wife, who were connected to the de Hochepied family.

The eldest of these two sons succeeded to the title in 1828 and his own son bought the South Devon County Hotel. Thus the name Larpent appears at two ends of the parish through two half brothers.

A granite cross was erected outside the church tower at Leusdon in memory of Charlotte Larpent. On its plinth is the inscription:

To the Glory of God
In memory of Charlotte Rosamund Larpent who built and endowed this church in 1863.
The memory of the just is blessed.

Bill Miners leads in the Old Grey Mare and Uncle Tom Cobley. (Bernard Miners)

Harvest break at Spitchwick – one of Dorothy Miners' memories of working on the land.
The figure at the back on the right is probably Edith Elizabeth French whilst the lady on the far left is
thought to be one of her sisters. (Hermon French Collection)

Chapter 2: Farming

❧ Bill Miners' Family ❧

Bill and Sam Miners were brothers who, after the First World War, worked together taking employment wherever it could be found. They are recorded in the Southcombe Diaries many times as members of shearing and threshing teams.   A contract with Devon County Council for road repairs saw them hiring a horse and cart from Southcombe, ripping out rocks from the nearest roadstone quarry and spreading them about where required, having physically cracked the rocks into smaller pieces leaving the iron-tyred cart traffic to crush the aggregate into a reasonable surface. From this humble beginning came two highly successful road-haulage businesses.

When the author knew them, Bill and his family lived at No.1 Lady Meadow Terrace while Sam and his family lived at No.5, and they would conduct their business at the top of their voices. Bill founded W.F. Miners & Sons, and Sam, who had married an employee's sister, formed Harris & Miners with his brother-in-law, Gerry Harris.

Stories about Bill and Sam abound, especially Bill, whose brushes with the authorities are legendary. This must have been the cause of some interesting situations because until they built a house, complete with cell, for the local bobby near the new school, the constable resided at No.2 Lady Meadow Terrace!

AGRICULTURAL CONTRACTING

Dorothy Baty (née Miners) writes:

I was fifteen when my father said he would like me to drive a tractor. He had a Land Army girl working for him... called Miss Fox. She took me out on my first day and showed me what to do, and then next day I was on my own. I was disc harrowing in a field on Broadaford... One did not need to pass a test in those days, but of course I was too young to drive on the road. Needless to say I did quite a lot.

The only farm I stayed at was Runnage, Postbridge, the home of the Coakers. I remember it was cold when I was there and the farmer's wife used to rub my hands to get them warm. The tractor was a Standard Fordson. We did work all around Widecombe, Princetown, Postbridge, Moretonhampstead, Bovey Tracey, Ilsington and many other places.

Bernard was only nine years old – he is six years younger than me, and came with me quite a lot.

Freda Wilkinson recalls riding past Broadaford and seeing 'what looked like a tractor and mower cutting grass without a driver, till I glimpsed a little gold head just bobbing up between the tractor wings. It was Bernard Miners.'

Dorothy says:

I worked with a two-furrow plough where it was rocky, elsewhere with a three-furrow. I remember my pride and joy was to keep the rows very straight. We worked from daylight until dark in the main season, and seven days a week. I never had any wages, I did not need a lot of money; when I did my father would give me some.

The harvest time was my favourite. I liked cutting the corn – no combine-harvester in those days, just a binder that tied the sheaves.   The farmer's wife would bring out a lovely tea and we would all sit around chatting.

I cannot remember the date, but a plane crashed on Hameldown and I had to go up with the tractor and tow a lot of the wreckage back. It was a bit of a trek as I had to miss all the big rocks on the way. I must have been about 18 or 19 at the time. I cannot remember how many were killed but a few years ago a memorial service was held up there. [This was the 50th anniversary service, on 25 August 1991, held for the four crew members, all of whom died on the night of 21 March l941.].

My mother was wonderful, she always had a meal waiting for us; sometimes it was very late.

Father bought a Fordson Major, it was quicker on the road than the Standard, about 12 miles an hour.

Dorothy Baty driving the tractor, spinning out potatoes. Her father is carrying the bucket and Bernard is behind her, c.1940. (Dorothy Baty)

Above: *Bernard Miners ready to drive his sister, Dorothy, to her wedding with Bill Baty, 1948.* (Dorothy Baty)

Left: *Passing Kernick's shop.* (Dorothy Baty)

The wedding group, 23 October 1948. (Dorothy Baty)
Children in front, left to right: Brian Harris, Mary Miners, Barry Baty, Sally Baty,
Heather Miners, Winnie Miners;
Standing behind, left to right: Bernard Miners, Brian Baty, William Baty senr, Bessie Baty senr,
Harry Heathman, Betty Baty, Fred Miners (holding Christine Miners), Bill Baty, Dorothy Baty, Jean Miners,
Joan Miners, Sheila Collings, Joyce Miners, Olive Miners, Olive E. Miners, Bill Miners, Ronald Collings,
Sam Miners, Daisy Miners.

Hameldown memorial stone.
(Elisabeth Stanbrook)

When we were cutting grass we had to take out the knives and sharpen them. The steepest field I ploughed was near Simms Hill, Ilsington [where] the tractor used to rear up in front and turn around. I must have had nerves of steel.

Bernard drove the tractor quite a lot, even on the roads. He once towed two trailers, one in front of the other through Bovey Tracey – how he got away with it I do not know, but of course there was not much traffic on the roads. Those were the days!

When I was 21 my boyfriend, Bill Baty, said to my father that we would like to get married. My father said he would like me to go to the church on the tractor and trailer. The tractor was the Standard that I used to drive. It was on 23 October 1948. It was a really lovely day with lots of sunshine. My uncle Sam and Fred Gough, the local thatcher, decorated the trailer. It's hard to believe it's our Golden Wedding this year. I loved driving the tractor; I was so used to the outdoor life it took me a time to settle afterwards.

Dorothy was the third of nine children, the others being: Freddie, Olive, Joan, Joyce, Bernard, Mary, Winnie, and Heather:

We were a very happy family, although it was very hard work for my mother. We had three bedrooms, my parents in one, the boys in one and all seven girls in the other. We had a bathroom with running cold water, but my mother had to light the copper to heat water and carry it upstairs when required. We had Aladdin lamps, later on gas lights, and later father was instrumental in getting mains electricity into Widecombe... mother did all the gardening.

I was in the Chapel choir with my sisters Joan, Joyce, Winnie and several other girls. We used to go across to the cottage, your [the author's] grandparents' home, to do Bible studies. I remember I did a test and passed with flying colours. Your grandparents were very good to us [and] we used to go on long walks with them through Buckland Woods to the junction of the Webburn and Dart. We always took a packed lunch.

Life has changed now [although] the moors are still beautiful. I love it when I get to the top of Widecombe Hill and look all around.

Bernard Miners, learning from his sister that the author was researching his family, wrote saying:

My father and his brother Sam went into business as W & S Miners. I was born in 1933 and remember the coal deliveries to all the schools in the area; Ashburton, Bovey, Buckfastleigh, Princetown, etc. You may not believe it, but I was delighted to stay home from school and hold the bags open and shovel the coal at the stations. My father also ran three taxis, a Minerva, an Austin 18 and an Austin 20. [There were] also cattle lorries and tippers (hand wound) working for the council around Widecombe. Earlier he had buses (without the seats), in which he carried cattle. I remember the first tractor with which we did contracting on the land from Princetown to Newton Abbot, Whiddon Down to South Brent. We increased the number of tractors to five. I was delighted to stay home to drive one (at nine years old).

I do not remember the horse-powered business, but remember sitting on the shafts behind Lion. Father then [bought] a model-T Ford [and] eventually we gave up the tractors and ran, at peak, 36 lorries out at Millbay Docks.

My father supported Widecombe in lots of ways; at Widecombe Fair riding the Old Grey Mare, with the Parish Council, as Chairman of Newton Abbot Rural District Council, Captain of the bellringers, a member of the famous tug-of-war team and a good supporter of the 'Old Inn'. Another achievement was blasting rock to dig wells as deep as 120 feet, and also the larger rocks in the fields. But his greatest triumph was bringing electricity to Widecombe.

The floodlit church commemorates the installation of mains electricity and (inset) Lily Hambley with Mr and Mrs Jim Hines (and unknown man on the right) switching on the electricity. (Julia Morley)

Clockwise
from above:
*Elizabeth Hannaford;
John Hannaford; Henry
Herbert Hannaford with
his wife Martha and two of
their children, John and
Marion* (all Elisabeth Stanbrook)*;
John Hannaford with his wife
Edith (who later married
Hermon French after John's
death); Marion with her
husband the Revd
Wood.*

❧ The Hannafords of Southcombe ❧

The author based his previous writings on farming on the information gleaned from studying the day-to-day diaries and notebooks kept by the Hannafords of Southcombe and Dockwell. If these recordings are extended through Edith French (*left*, who married John Hannaford and, after his death, married Hermon French) the diaries cover the period from 1896 to 1968.

There being many Hannafords in Widecombe's history, the author decided to concentrate on the family of John Hannaford of Southcombe and on the family of his son, Henry Herbert Hannaford. John died on 15 December 1874 aged 72 years. A quick glance at the Parish Registers leaves one staring the genealogical abyss of Widecombe in the face:

1801
Hanaford, Elizabeth,   *d. of John and Elizabeth*
10 Jan
Hannaford, Betsey,   *d. of Thomas and Mary*
3 May
Hannaford, Roger,   *s. of John and Elizabeth*
20 May
Hannaford, Thomas,   *s. of William and Ann*
15 June
Hannaford, Betsey,   *d. of John and Susanna*
29 June
Hannaford, Richard,   *s. of Robert and Elizabeth*
7 July

1802
Hannaford, John,   *s. of Roger and Joan*
11 May
Hannaford, John,   *s. of John and Nancy*
1 June
Hannaford, John,   *s. of Samuel and Elizabeth*
1 June

Here we see three Johns born in 1802, two on the same day, and with seven different Hannaford families recorded in the two years. It has been said that there were once 11 families bearing this name in the parish, although none survive today.

John Hannaford had two brothers; Roger, who emigrated to America, and Samuel, to whom John lent money when he went into farming for himself.

The Parish Registers show the following:

1805
Hannaford, Roger,   *s. of John and Nancy*
9 Jan
1807
Hannaford, Samuel,   *s. of John and Nancy*
21 Apr
1809
Hannaford, Dinah,   *d. of John and Nancy*
22 Aug

This clan of Hannafords over two generations epitomised the structure of land-owning families during the 19th and early 20th centuries. The farm would support a husband and wife plus growing children and the eldest son could expect to work on the farm and eventually to receive it as it passed from father to son. Daughters could marry, but other sons had to make their own way, seeking work elsewhere and often, during this period, emigrating. And so it was with Roger Hannaford. Close to his 40th birthday he and his wife Mary sailed from Liverpool to America, where on arrival he posted on numerous letters he had taken with him from English friends and acquaintances who had loved ones on the other side of the Atlantic. His first letter home is dated 19 November 1844 and is the first of a series that survive written by himself to his brothers and, later, his cousins. The folio continues with letters sent in turn by his children to their cousins.

Roger Hannaford did not make his fortune; he managed reasonably well at farming and was very religious, being active in one of the Free Churches. Among the surviving music books of Widecombe Church Bands is a school exercise book in which Roger had included hymns from America and compositions that he himself had written.

His wife Mary was very ill in 1852 and a letter to Henry Herbert Hannaford from Roger's daughter, Maggie, in 1887, suggests that Mary must have died and Roger remarried:

Dear Cousin Herbert
I wrote you a few weeks ago of Father's sickness so you are somewhat prepared for the sad news I have to tell you. Our Dear Father died last Tuesday Sept 20th (1887) at 4 o'clock P.M... it is thirty four years Oct 4th since Father and Mother married.

Maggie had previously written on 7 August 1884 to her cousin Martha (Henry Herbert's wife) saying:

Henry Herbert Hannaford and the frontispiece and extracts from the Southcombe Diaries for February 1920, the month of his death.
(Elisabeth Stanbrook)

'Father kept the group. We think Marion is just as cute and pretty as she can be and that John is a sweet little fellow.' Elisabeth Stanbrook purchased a Hannaford photo album at a sale and allowed the author to reproduce some of its contents, including the picture of this group (*see page 36*).

In 1864 John Hannaford recorded 'An account of what Samuel had of me when going into business on Bullaton Farm' (from where he may later have moved to Hatchwell):

	£	s	d
Cash to buy Furniture	28	7	1
A Trap	4	5	0
135 Sheep and Lambs	200	0	0
Six Cows and Calfs	63	0	0
Four young Bullocks	24	0	0
Six yearling Bullocks	24	0	0
Three Horses and One Colt	40	0	0
One Breeding Sow	2	10	0
One Fat Pig about 20 score at 9/-	9	0	0
Nine bags of seed wheat	4	14	6
Twenty-nine bags of seed Oats 6/3	9	3	6
Five bags of seed barley at 7/6	1	17	6
Thrashing Machine	34	0	0
Cart and Harness	6	0	0
Two ploughs and three pair of Harrows	6	9	0
Six new Hemp bags and some old ones	1	15	0
Scarrifier Scuffle and Chain Harrow	4	0	0
Forty Eight bags of Seed Potatoes 3/6	8	8	0
Two new Horse Collars, two old ones, Harness and other Horse Tackling	2	10	0
Wheelbarrow		10	6
Several empty Casks	2	10	0
Sundry Tools such as Mattocks, Shovels, Rakes, Prongs	1	0	0
120 Hurdels at 6d	3	0	0
Wheat for family use from Lady Day to the end of October at 5 pecks a week, 31 weeks, 19 bags at 12/- a bag	11	8	0
About 10 bags of Potatoes for family use	1	10	0
Table and Form in back kitchen		7	6
Total	494	5	7

John and Elizabeth Hannaford had at least one child, Henry Herbert Hannaford, who was born on 9 June 1846 and died on 12 February 1920. He married Matha Lambshead who was born on 6 September 1849 and died on 22 May 1902, a day which is marked in the diary, as previously mentioned, with a simple cross. Henry Herbert and Martha had five children; Marion, John, Sam, Nancy and Martha. Henry Herbert was a working farmer but also an active part of community life. His gravestone tells us that he was a 'Justice of the Peace for the County of Devon'. He also aspired to be a County Councillor, for which position he was nominated on 26 February 1919 by J. Foaden and W. Abbot. He also held the posts of Reeve for Widecombe Town Manor and Foreman of the Jury for Dunstone and Blackslade Manor and was on the committee for the Methodist Chapels at Poundsgate and Dunstone.

Marion Hannaford (1883-1956) was Henry and Martha's eldest child. The 1919 diary records the vicar as being a frequent visitor to Southcombe, so that it comes as no surprise to read on 10 June:

H.H.H. to the wedding and drove Shamrock to Ilsington. Marion married to Rev. E.C. Wood... John, Ethel and Mollie Loveys, Mr and Mrs J.S. Neck and family and Sam and Emily Hannaford and Ernest and Carrie Walters, and May Dunning and Jamie Lambshead here also J. and A. Lambshead: Fan Lambshead, H. and A. Wills at Church.

The Revd Elliot Colpoys Wood was vicar of Widecombe for a great many years, but Marion's brother John was not over pleased with her choice probably because Revd Wood was so much older. Jack Prouse remembers that:

After his death she had to leave the Vicarage so she bought Heatherbank. She was eccentric to say the least! It was not unusual for anyone invited to tea to find... she had forgotten all about it. Her egg sandwiches were often complete with eggshells.

John Hannaford (1884-1931) was the eldest son and, as previously stated, is mentioned by his father on the frontispiece of the 1902 diary as being the 'Clerk of the Works'. Although the diaries are written in many different hands it can be seen that he took the job seriously by the diligent manner in which the diaries were kept.

After his father's death John shouldered many local responsibilities. Jack Prouse who remembers him wrote, saying:

John Hannaford of Southcombe, commonly known as Janny Hannaford, I remember him, not a very big man in stature. He had a severe physical deformity. He had small hands that he usually held about waist high and they pointed towards each other. Both hands were very deformed and holding anything was a great effort. As far as I can remember his walking was also rather difficult. His usual means of transportation around the village and local area was a pony and trap. The trap was what we called a 'jingle', a square body that would hold say four people. It was not very high off the ground

Wedding of Marion Hannaford to Revd Wood, vicar of Widecombe. Henry Herbert Hannaford is standing next to his daughter. The bridesmaids could be Phyllis and Linda French.

The family of Edith Elizabeth Hannaford (née French), wife of Hermon French (inset, at boarding school), to whom she was married after the death of John Hannaford. Left to right, back: Herbert John, Edith Elizabeth, Hermon, Thirza (mother), Jasper; in front: Nancy, John Herbert (father), Betty.

Edith French on her way from Southcombe to Dockwell.

and for entry had a step and hinged door at the back. I can remember him sitting very hunched up in the jingle and holding the reins with his deformed hands. He was, amongst other things, a member of the local council and a school manager.

John Hannaford married Edith Elizabeth French, so it is not surprising to see 'Miss E.E. French here' in the diary, which changed to 'EEF here' and, sometimes, to 'E'. The couple married at Poundsgate Chapel and went to Torquay for their honeymoon.

Nancy Agnes Hannaford was the fourth child (1889-1895) and she does not appear in the diaries. Elisabeth Stanbrook has her portrait but all that appears to be known of her is recorded on her grandfather's tombstone:

In memory of John Hannaford of Southcombe who died Dec. 15th 1874 aged 72 years. Also of Elizabeth his wife who died Dec. 28th 1889 aged 78 years. Also Nancy Agnes Hannaford granddaughter of the above who died April 20th 1895, aged 5 years and 11 months.

Martha Hannaford (1891-1920) was the fifth child. She is recorded in the diaries, was frequently sick and visiting the doctor, but she did all the things a Dartmoor child might do, riding a pony, swaling, and whortleberry picking. But tragedy was to hit the family when Martha died, for we read:

Wed 11th Feb.1920, H.H.H to Newton, Matty died. Thursday 12th, H.H.H to Dunstone and Widecombe and around farm. Father died suddenly at about 11 pm.'

Matty's death seemed to have broken her father's heart and it would also seem that he knew of his imminent end and went out to look one final time at Widecombe, his cottage at Dunstone (Tremills) and to walk around the farm he had lived on for 73 years. His tombstone reads: 'After he had served his own generation by the Will of God fell on sleep and was laid unto his fathers.'

Samuel Hannaford (1886-1936) was the third child and second son and, like his great uncle Roger, decided to emigrate, choosing to go to Australia. His father wrote to him and each letter is numbered, revealing Samuel's nomadic existence:

1911
Posted letter No.39 to Sam at Fredale.
Posted letter No.55 to Sam at Brisbane.
Posted letter No.79 to Sam at Helidon.

In 1915 a new address is recorded: 'S.Hannaford No.2154, D Company, 9 Battalion, 3 Brigade, Alexandria, Egypt.' On 16 June 1916 Sam arrived at Plymouth and went on to Wiltshire, arriving in Widecombe on 15 July. He was ordered to France on 28 August 1917. He returned to Australia in 1818, where he died on 30 August 1936.

Workers, thought to be Hermon French (top) and Sam Cannon, haymaking. (Hermon French Collection)

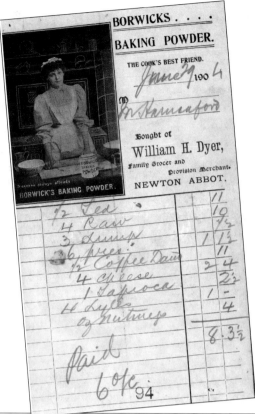

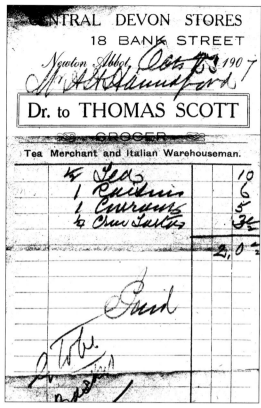

RULES FOR CALCULATING

the weight of potatoes per acre from the weight of a single stalk: weigh the stalk in ounces: divide by 3 & the answer is in Tons per acre for potatoes planted 18" apart in drills 29¼" apart: for calculation of an "ideal" crop from a single large potato × by 10 & divide by 3 as before.

To calculate the weight of an "ideal" crop of wheat:— weigh the contents of a single ear or take the average of say 10 ears, in 60 ozs: answer will be also in Tons per acre, for a seeding of 153½ lbs per acre & 2 ears of wheat per plant if all grow to harvest. Meccanonuts = 60 oz each.

To calculate weight of roots per acre from small plot take a frame 50" by 56": weigh crop inside frame in lbs = Tons per acre.

To calculate weight of potatoes per acre from weight of 1 row, × length of row in yards by 5 & ÷ by 6. divide this into 4840 & × by weight of potatoes in lbs.
Alternative way: there are 5808 yds of row in 1 acre ∴ divide length of row into 5808 & × by weight of potatoes in lbs.

To calculate weight of roots per acre from any row: weigh the produce of 140 inches of row (after F. Shull) in lbs: the answer is in Tons per acre: for any other drill the length of row to be taken will be 2800 ÷ by width between two drills in inches.

Above, left and right: *Receipts received by Mr and Mrs H. H. Hannaford for groceries bought from Devon Central Stores and William H. Dyer of Newton Abbot in 1904 and 1907.*

Left: *Hermon French's various methods used to calculate the weights of potatoes, wheat and roots per acre.*

❧ From the Hermon ❧ French Collection

Above: Hand cut and stacked.

Above: *Cutting hay.*
Right: *Thatching the rick.*
Far right: *Hand-rearing a piglet.*
Below: *A welcome break.*

❧ Deborah Hannaford's Collection ❧

*Deborah is of the Natsworthy Hannafords who are
unrelated to those of Southcombe and Dockwell*

Above: *Clockwise from top:
Miss Ada Nosworthy, Mrs
Elizabeth Hannaford, Miss
Rose Hannaford, c.1911.*

Top right: *Geoffrey Hannaford setting out for
Widecombe Fair where his horse won first prize,
1948.*

Above: *Marie Hannaford and friends, Lower
Natsworthy.*

Above left: *Charlie (left) and Ted Hannaford
(right) stacking the last of the corn.*

Left: *Hayrick, 29 August 1965.*

The wedding of Mr and Mrs Dowrick, 1937.

A Hannaford wedding, 1936. Left to right, back: Richard Hannaford, Charlie Hannaford, Elsie Hannaford (née Irish), Deborah Hannaford; front: Enid Chaffe, Louise Nosworthy.

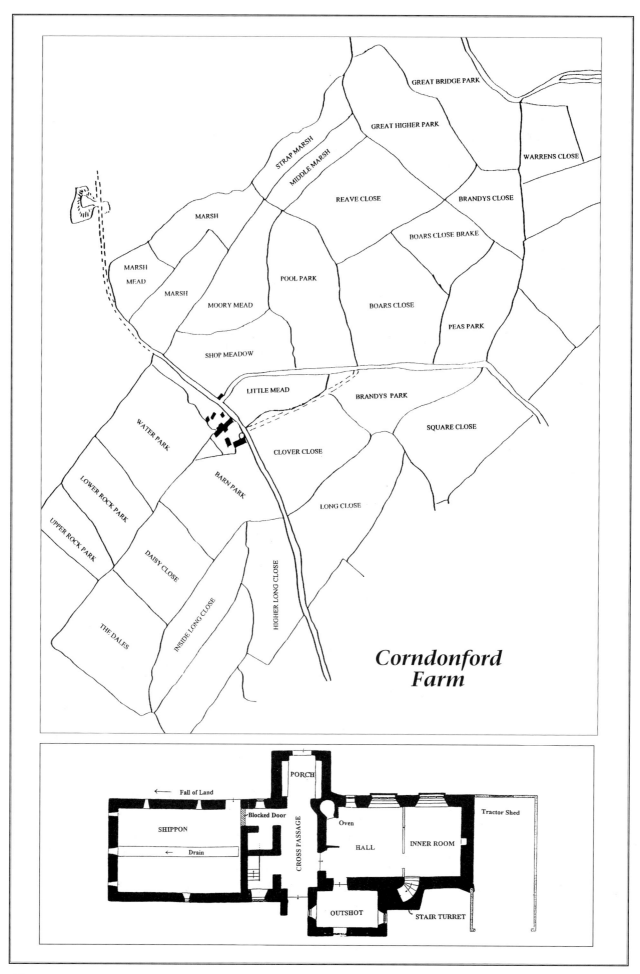

Corndonford Farm

GREAT BRIDGE PARK
GREAT HIGHER PARK
WARRENS CLOSE
STRAP MARSH
MIDDLE MARSH
REAVE CLOSE
BRANDYS CLOSE
MARSH
BOARS CLOSE BRAKE
MARSH MEAD
POOL PARK
BOARS CLOSE
MARSH
MOORY MEAD
PEAS PARK
SHOP MEADOW
LITTLE MEAD
BRANDYS PARK
SQUARE CLOSE
WATER PARK
CLOVER CLOSE
LOWER ROCK PARK
BARN PARK
LONG CLOSE
UPPER ROCK PARK
DAISY CLOSE
THE DALES
INSIDE LONG CLOSE
HIGHER LONG CLOSE

PORCH
Fall of Land
Blocked Door
SHIPPON
CROSS PASSAGE
Oven
Tractor Shed
Drain
HALL
INNER ROOM
OUTSHOT
STAIR TURRET

Corndonford

Since the publication of the author's first volume on Widecombe, the late Elizabeth Gawne's painstaking research into Widecombe longhouses has also been printed, and those who want to know more about these fascinating buildings should read her excellent work.

The author has chosen to look at this subject by studying the farm known as Corndonford, earlier recorded as Upper Corndon, there being a Corndon Farm near by. It is a particularly interesting longhouse, not least because of the Bronze Age reave or wall which runs down the flank of the Corndon and appears to follow the back wall of the farmhouse, begging the question – could the foundations be made from stones placed there by Bronze-Age labourers? It would be nice to think so, but nobody knows for sure. Corndonford is also made special by the fact that the present owner, Ann Williams, is a heavy-horse enthusiast and uses the horse power of Leo and Lupin (*above*) to cultivate her fields, a method that died out in the parish more than 40 years ago.

Leo and Lupin competing on the common below Southsea Castle.

The Turners farmed Corndonford for most of the 20th century using the basic methods of cultivation and animal husbandry believed to have been in practice since written history on Widecombe began and which, thanks to Bessie French (née Turner), remain preserved for future generations in an excellent photographic record of life on the farm.

In January 1994, the National Park had a survey made by John Pigeon and, based on this, Deborah Griffiths, Head of Archaeology and Historic Buildings of the DNPA (Dartmoor National Park Authority), has written the following account:

Widecombe Parish boasts some of the best examples of the longhouse on Dartmoor and Corndonford is one of this notable group. The longhouse is most succinctly described as a building which housed people and animals under the same roof. A long, relatively narrow rectangular structure, it was built into a hillside and so sloped, or stepped down, from one end to the other. The longhouse was effectively divided into two halves by a passage across its width, at each end of which was a door to the
outside. On the lower side of the cross passage was the shippon, where cattle were housed during the winter months and on the higher side the living quarters of the farmer and his family. Corndonford is a rare member of the family of longhouses in that it has a decorated stone door frame to the porch, but also in that it has escaped having the shippon end converted at some time in the past to domestic use.

Most longhouses appear to have begun life as single-storey structures, with an open hearth in the main living room, called the hall. The most common evidence for this is the survival of medieval roof trusses, blackened by smoke from the open fire. Unfortunately at Corndonford, the roof timbers were replaced in the 18th century and so the date and original form of the farmhouse are unclear. However, the likelihood is that the farmhouse originated as a late-medieval, single-storey longhouse, comprising the hall, with an inner room beyond, a cross passage and a shippon at the lower end.

This being the case, subsequent (i.e. 16-17th century) development would have included the addition of fireplaces with chimney stacks and the insertion of first-floor rooms over the hall, inner room and possibly the cross passage. The hall fireplace is set with its back to the cross passage and has an ashlared (dressed block) granite rear wall, with a corbel table at ceiling level. This is a sophisticated, prestigious (and probably relatively expensive) architectural element meant to be seen and appreciated. Outside, the stack above ridge level is also made of granite ashlar. At some later point, but before the beginning of the 18th century, a bread oven was inserted into the right-hand side of the fireplace, its wall bulging into the cross passage. The hall was lit by two windows in the front (SE) wall of the building, one with granite lintel and sill.

The inner room was also lit by a window in the front wall; here too, at some time in the 16th or 17th century, a fireplace and stack were inserted in the end wall. Access to the first-floor rooms was (and indeed still is) by way of a spiral stone staircase, whose turret projects out from the rear wall of the inner room.

A relatively common addition to longhouses was a porch on the principal elevation. This gave protection to the entrance and provided additional

A group in 1924 at Leusdon School, which Bessie French (née Turner) attended from Corndonford.
Left to right, back: Eleanor French (teacher), Frank Burgess, Leslie White, Phyllis Norrish,
Charlie French, Helen Hannaford, Gordon Smale, Harold Cambridge, Miss Brin (head teacher);
centre: Jack Burgess, Evelyn Norrish, Thirza Caunter, Clifford White, Catherine French,
Stanley French, Rosemarie Hazel, ?;
front: Grace Lane, Gladys French, Joan Warren, Margaret and Evelyn Tall, Bessie Turner, Molly Heywood.
The name Thirza is surprisingly common in Widecombe; it became popular with many people after its
appearance in a novel of the early 19th century about Cain and Abel.

A 1907 photograph by Chapman & Son of Townwood, Poundsgate – birthplace (in 1909) of Bessie's
husband, John French. (Kath Brewer)

Above: *A typical Dartmoor fireplace with a settle on the right. Ann Williams of Corndonford used the old floorboards to create a settle for herself when the longhouse was renovated.* (Chapman & Son)

Above: *Great-grandmother of Bessie French, Grannie White at Sherwell with her grandson Leslie.* (Bessie French)

Right: *Edwin (left) and Richard Turner or Corndonford Farm.* (Bessie French)

Right: *Edwin Turner sharpening his scythe, 1932.* (Bessie French)

Above: *Bessie's uncle, Richard Turner, and Gladys Turner with Scot the dog, 1933.* (Bessie French)

Corndonford Farm. (Bessie French)

accommodation at first floor level. It also gave another opportunity to make an overt display of quality workmanship. Perhaps about half a dozen 17th-century porches on Dartmoor longhouses have round-headed granite doorways, with patterns and often a date carved in the spandrels (the stonework immediately above the head and sides of the arch). The porch at Corndonford is possibly later than most of our dated examples: within a pattern of fleur-de-lis and shields is inscribed 'RW' on one spandrel and '1718' on the other. Five rectangular pigeon holes set in a row high up on the NE side wall of the porch are probably later insertions.

At roughly the same time as the porch was first constructed (the early 18th century), it seems that a new roof was put over the higher end of the longhouse (c.f. above); this might have been associated with a raising of the ridge line, which would have given greater height – and comfort – in the first-floor rooms.

The shippon in a longhouse is normally characterised by a drain running lengthways down the centre of the ground floor, which lets out through a small hole in the end wall. Above this is commonly found a square opening, used to eject dung and straw from the inside. Other openings are narrow slits, which although splayed inwards, must have provided rather poor light and ventilation. All of these features are present at Corndonford, except that the shippon here seems to be a rebuild – probably of the 19th century. The alignment of the shippon is different from that of the main part of the house and its walls are thinner and more regular.

All the internal timberwork is 19th-century or later.

With the re-building of the shippon, the opportunity appears to have been taken to widen the cross passage into part of the area formerly occupied by the shippon, thus allowing for the creation of one or two small rooms on the lower side of the passage and an enlarged first-floor room over. Examples of a separate door into the shippon from the outside can be found in 16th- and 17th-century longhouses elsewhere on Dartmoor, so the one here is not unusual. One important aspect of the longhouse is that access can be gained from the living area to the shippon via a door in the cross passage. This element was retained in the rebuilt shippon at Corndonford, but the doorway, located towards the front of the building, was subsequently blocked and the traditional relationship between people and animals ceased.

The final major phase of development (in the mid-late 19th century) was the addition of a small lean-to, known as an outshot, to the rear of the hall. The pitch of the main roof has been continued downwards to cover this small extension. Again, outshots are to be found at many longhouses; they would probably have been used as a dairy or larder, with, if two-storied like the one at Corndonford, a small bedroom above.

Thus in many ways, Corndonford is a typical Dartmoor longhouse, but there are features within it that make it unique. As with many of our traditional buildings, the complete story of its origins and development may never be known – but many would say that the mystery adds to the charm.

THE BARN

Opposite the front of the longhouse, across the yard, is a late 18th- or early 19th-century threshing barn, stone built with a slate roof. There is a double doorway, slightly off-centre, in the front elevation of the barn. In the back wall, directly opposite this, is a single doorway. Between the two would have been the threshing floor, where the grain of the harvested cereals would have been separated from the straw using hand flails. The large double doorway would have allowed access for carts bringing the cereals in from the fields; the crops would then have been stored in the rest of the building to await threshing. Successful threshing relied upon a draught of air to blow away the chaff; and this is the purpose of the single doorway at the rear. Later barns tended to have a double doorway on each side, perhaps to make for easier cart access.

The 19th century saw increased mechanisation on the farm and hand flailing was supplanted by the threshing machines; some of these were portable and used in the fields, but others were stationary and commonly housed in the barn. At Corndonford, the threshing machine would have stood at the roadside end of the building. The power for driving the threshing machine was provided by a horse, attached to a horse engine or gin, located on the outside of the barn and therefore divided from the threshing machine by the barn wall. The horse, by walking in a circle around the engine, would cause a central vertical spindle to rotate and this in turn would drive an overhead horizontal shaft which passed through an opening in the barn wall and into the threshing machine. The horse engine at Corndonford was enclosed in a semi-circular structure, known, perhaps not altogether unsurprisingly, as a horse engine house, or a round house. The walls of this now roofless building still survive, as does the hole in the barn wall through which the horizontal shaft passed. There is a large gap in the wall of the round house on the yard side; this was to allow air to circulate inside the building and prevent the horse from becoming overheated.

Top: *Bessie French's mother, Elsie Turner (née Irish) of Grendon, at the Corndonford trough.* (Bessie French)
Above: *Bessie's brother Alec (to the right) and her father Edwin standing in front of the barn at Corndonford.*

ARCHAEOLOGY

Within a radius of about a third of a mile of the farmstead of Corndonford, are three deserted medieval settlements. One, Dinna Clerks, to the north of Corndonford, was excavated in the 1960s by an amateur archaeologist from Torquay, Mrs Minter. Here are the remains of a single-storey longhouse, built around AD1250 and abandoned at the end of the 14th or early 15th century. Mrs Minter believed that the building had been destroyed by fire. Due west of the farmstead, on the eastern slopes of Corndon Down, are the remains of another single-storey building, unexcavated, but probably a longhouse and probably of much the same date as Dinna Clerk's. The same might be said of the three buildings situated in a small enclosure to the east of Corndonford, near Corndon Farm.

The place name of Corndon first appears in documentary records in 1303. There is therefore good evidence for medieval settlement in the area and of farming activity for over 700 years. However, the agricultural landscape is far more ancient than that. Up on Corndon Down is a well-preserved and extensive area of abandoned pre-historic fields, which forms part of what is known as the Dartmeet reave system. Reaves are the name given to the stony field boundaries created around the middle of the second millennium BC, when Dartmoor was comparatively intensely settled and farmed. Over 10 000 hectares (25 000 acres) of pre-historic fields survive on the lower contours of Dartmoor. What is especially characteristic about the reaves is that they run parallel to one another, forming long narrow fields. On the southern side of Corndon Down, the reaves run in a NNE direction, but then dog-legs towards the North East. A glance at a map showing the present-day farmland around Corndonford Farm, will show that many of the field boundaries here also run from SW to NE. They have, in fact, been built on top of the prehistoric reaves and are therefore some 3500 years old. This makes them amongst some of the oldest field boundaries in the country.

ECOLOGICAL INTEREST OF CORNDONFORD FARM AND THE ADJACENT COMMON

Wet pastures along the north-western edge of the farm are very rich in wild flowers and associated insects. For example, nationally rare or uncommon species such as Pale Butterwort, Ivy-leaved Bellflower, Marsh Plume Thistle, Creeping Willow and Sawwort can be found here along with butterflies including the Small Pearl-bordered Fritillary, Dark Green Fritillary and the nationally threatened Marsh Fritillary. The total area of species-rich pasture amounts to only 35 hectares (9 acres), but contains at least 134 different species of flowering plants. The boggy fields also contain a good population of frogs and several dragonfly species, including the nationally scarce Keeled Skimmer. The whole site was considered to be of outstanding nature conservation importance in a recent survey of Rhos pastures on Dartmoor carried out by the National Park Authority.

The common land lying to the north of the farm is important, for two nationally restricted insect species survive there. The scarce Blue-tailed Damselfly is found in the wet runnels which form part of the same wetland system as the fields referred to above. A small colony of Pearl-bordered Fritillaries exists on the bracken-covered slopes of the common where the foodplant of its caterpillar, the Dog Violet, is to be found.

Edwin Turner in Corndon Close pulling mangels. (Bessie French)

Haymakers at Middle Cator Farm, 1951. Left to right: Mr Alfred Bovey senr (Miss Bovey is hidden behind him), Peter Hannaford, Edwin Turner, Alec Turner, William 'Bill' Bovey (father), Ethel Bovey (mother), Gilbert Sercombe and his wife Cynthia (William and Ethel's daughter who came with her husband from Loddiswell to help her parents with the harvest. (photograph taken by Cynthia's sister Brenda M. Bovey)

❧ Lower Cator Farm ❧

Left: *This is believed to be Mrs Irish at Lower Cator.*
Above: *Mrs Irish (left) in the farmyard, 1915.*
(Bessie French)

Irish family silver wedding at Lower Cator. (Marjorie and Geoff Weymouth)
Left to right, back: Thirza, Francis, John, Louie, Ruth, Bessie;
front: Walter, Ethel, Edmund (father), Bessie (mother);
with cat: Elsie.

❧ The Red and White Tide of Agistment ❧

The commons and Dartmoor Forest have long provided a good habitat for sheep, cattle and ponies, thanks to their excellent pastures, abundance of clean water throughout the seasons and careful swaling to regenerate the verbage. Widecombe farmers used this pasturage in the summer for their flocks of sheep and it was recorded by Charles Vancouver in 1808 that an estimated 14 000 sheep could be found on the commons of Widecombe. Nowadays, numbers would struggle to reach a tenth of that figure, although some believe the moor to be over grazed.

But if numbers seem to have once been high, there was an ancient restriction which commanded that the number of stock being de-pastured had to match the number that could be supported on the farm over winter. When this excellent piece of husbandry came about is not clear; it could have been as early as Saxon times but is usually categorised as 'tyme out of minde'. As a result of the condition, the Widecombe farmer would have fields in the Kingsbridge district, Ipplepen, Sparnham or even Marldon. Sylvester Mann informed the author that he would spend every day and night of the three-week lambing season with his flock at Marldon and then, when the time was right, would bring them up to Mead Hill, rest the night and on the following day drive them on to Stannon Newtake for the summer.

Farmers of the in country meanwhile would work the other way around; they had herds of cattle that wintered on their farms but sought to make use of the Forest pasture and abundant water by putting their animals into the care of the moorman and his herdsmen who lived and worked on the high moors – a procedure known as agistment.

In 1935 11-year-old John Hooper worked for Adolphus Coaker of Runnage on Saturdays and during school holidays. He lived at Higher Pizwell Farm where his family farmed for 37 years from 1935 to 1972 and went to school at Postbridge where he was taught by the notable Miss Ladd (who never failed to get every pupil through the 11-plus examinations). On the last Saturday in May John was ready for work at 5.30 a.m. Together with Adolphus and four or five other

Sam Caunter of Sweaton Farm, Ponsworthy.
(Barbara Norrish)

herdsmen, he made his way to the green at Denbury. Here farmers who wanted to put cattle out on the moor for the summer had gathered together a large herd (usually between 250 and 500 head, although on one occasion the number was nearer 2000).

In those days it might take an animal three to four years to reach maturity – compared with today's figure of around 18 months – and some of the cattle would have been going up on to the moor for the second or third time.

With the herd under way the red tide soon stretched out along the highway heading towards the moor. The journey took them up Halsanger, Cold East Cross, Cockingford, down Church Lane, turning up past Southcombe to Blackaton past Grendon and on to Runnage. It was quite often the case that when the first steers reached Runnage the back markers were still heading for Grendon. The cattle were mustered 25 at a time in a square stone pen which made for a very tight fit. The men then walked across the animals' backs cutting a cross on the horn of each animal. Each farmer branded his own cattle on the horn and hoof, Adolphus Coaker's collective mark being an X.

With branding completed the herd moved off for their summer pasture. Adolphus Coaker leased the Stannon Newtakes from the Duchy and Jim Endacott of Chagford was the Duchy moorman responsible for the repair of the walls, gates and for swaling when and where necessary.

Once the stock were secured inside the newtake the men could head home; often this was after darkness had fallen. John Hooper had certainly earned his half crown (12 pence) the hard way and he also knew that the following three Saturdays would be spent repeating the process.

Some farmers elected to have their heifers run with a bull and Adolphus provided an excellent South Devon bull as part of the service. These animals were usually penned together in Little Stannon Newtake. The charges were 5 shillings on the Forest and 7s.6d. for those penned with the bull.

If any animals escaped or wandered off they had to be found and brought back. John recalls

George French in front of the gate to Pizwell House, 1892. (Robert Burnard)

Olive and Dorothy Burnard outside the middle house at Pizwell (formerly Pushyll) and (inset) Pizwell in 1889. (Robert Burnard)

accompanying Adolphus Coaker all the way to Lydford to collect strays. Sylvester Mann had a pony which was taken to Bampton Fair for sale by lorry and then to Tavistock by its new owner. So fond was it of Widecombe, however, that it turned up the following year back at Great Dunstone.

In September the process was reversed and the animals were driven back to Denbury. As they approached the end of their journey the farmers would start to separate their own animals from the herd and agistment for the year was over.

Sylvia Needham says that the moormen rode sturdy horses a good 14 hands high which were often part thoroughbred but that farmers rode them in a very informal style, simply sitting astride any old how and that they were very bow legged from the hours they spent in the saddle. She had dealings with Jim Smith of Hexworthy, (brother to Jack, George and Alec) who managed agistment in that part of the moor. Sylvia bought cattle from Jim when she farmed Broadaford, and Mr Dracup who farms there now still has that strain in his herd today.

The great white tide was formed by the flocks of sheep being brought up to eat on the high moorland pasture. Sylvester Mann remembers when the white tide stretched from New Bridge all the way to Leusdon Common. He had a flock which numbered 200 and his father and uncles had also run large flocks, but the Caunters of Sweaton and Langdons of Bittleford both had flocks which numbered 1000 or more.

Because so many sheep resided on the Forest or in the Stannon Newtakes a sheep dip was built there to meet the requirements of the law concerning the control of scab and other diseases. Sheep were charged by the score and many years ago one per score would wear a bell to help with the counting.

Gladys Mann remarked to the author that a farmer would use his knife on sheep foot rot, then cut a fresh carrot or turnip for his children – they never seemed to die, get ill or go to the doctor's!

Canon Hall reminisced with Iris Woods about 'Old Caunter' of Sweaton, who wintered his sheep at Chillington in the South Hams. When asked whether he drove home from there, he replied in the negative. Neither, it transpired, did he walk: 'I came jiggity', he explained, 'you don't run and you don't walk, you lollop. I jiggitied all the way home, always stopped and had a glass of white ale and when the pubs shut I came on and got back about 2 o'clock [a.m.].' When asked which he route he took, Sam named places that are just lanes now, but which described an almost straight line all the way.

Sylvester Mann says that it was a common practice, carried out by his father and uncle, for one to ride a mile and then tether the horse while the other would walk to the waiting animal, mount and ride on past the other one before himself tethering the horse a mile ahead and continuing on foot. By this method, both rode and walked half the journey. He also related how his father would be out hoeing turnips, would stop his work, ride to Torquay on business, return and go straight back to his hoeing without so much as a break.

*A flock of sheep following each other up onto Riddon Ridge and (*inset*) Riddon Ridge under attack from fire.*

Sam Caunter. (Thirza Nosworthy)

Sheep on the move.

South Devon Cattle, c.1950.

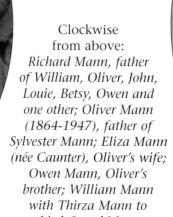

Mann Family

Clockwise
from above:
*Richard Mann, father
of William, Oliver, John,
Louie, Betsy, Owen and
one other; Oliver Mann
(1864-1947), father of
Sylvester Mann; Eliza Mann
(née Caunter), Oliver's wife;
Owen Mann, Oliver's
brother; William Mann
with Thirza Mann to
his left and Mary
Caunter to his
right.*

❧ Widecombes ❦

Sylvester Mann *(left, as a child)* recalls that the sheep known today as White-faced Dart-moors were, in his youth, referred to as Widecombes. Other breeds such as the Scotch Blackface and Cheviot are also to be found on the moors.

A farmer's flock was a very important factor in the local econo-my. On smallholdings one or two score might be kept, running sometimes to 200 or 300 and, on a small number of farms, the count would reach 1000. The animals were kept for both the excellent taste of their meat and for the fleece.

The stock check after lambing at Southcombe taken on 31 March 1905 recorded 120 living lambs: 35 doubles and 50 singles as well as 27 dead. There were 97 ewes, 98 hogs and one ram giving a total of 316 animals. The sheep were kept on the commons in summer, on the farm at lamb-ing and on fields owned at Sparnham during the winter. John Hannaford of Southcombe kept a detailed list of the sales of wool and the price per pound received:

	P	Q	lb		£	s	d
1854	1	1	7	at 7³/₄ d. (per lb)	9	15	0
1855	2	1	2	at 9d.	20	6	6
1856	2	3	18	at 11d.	31	1	6
1857	3	0	57	at 1s.1d.	42	1	9
1858	4	3	33	at 1s.0d.	58	13	0
1859	5	2	10	at 1¹/₂ d.	69	5	5
1860	5	0	53	at 1s.1d.	73	1	10
1861	5	0	43	at 1s.1d. and ¹/₂ farthing	68	2	7
1862	5	3	6	at 1¹/₂ d.	77	19	3
1863	6	3	13	at 1s.3d.	102	1	3
1864	4	3	56	at 1s.6¹/₂ d.	92	3	0
1865	4	3	56	at 1s.5d.	84	14	0
1866	10	3	45	at 9d.	98	8	9
1867							
1868	6	0	54	at 10³/₄ d.	66	18	4
1869	7	1	2	at 10d. and ¹/₂ farthing	76	4	0
1870	6	2	6	at 10d.	65	5	0
1871	5	1	14	at 1s.5¹/₂ d.	92	15	6
1872	6	3	24	at 1s.5d.	116	8	0
1873	8	1	40	at 1s.2¹/₄ d.	120	1	0
1874	8	1	51	at 1s.	101	11	0
1875	16	2	10	at 10¹/₂ d.	173	3	9
1876							

The author studied John Hannaford's record and tried to work out its values. P could refer to pack and Q to quarter (not the usual 28lb but with a weight over 57lb). A call to Freda Wilkinson produced an interesting set of wool weights, the final two of which (in bold) seem to match those used by John Hannaford:

7lb	=	*1 Clove*		*12 Sack*	=	*1 Last*
1 Clove	=	*1 Stone*		*1 Pack*	=	*240lb*
2 Stone	=	*1 Pod:*	***Ergo:***	***Quarter***	=	***60lb***
6¹/₂ Pods	=	*1 Wey*	***And:***	***¹/₂ farthing***	=	***1 mite.***

'The Shearers', from Dartmoor Snapshots, Beatrice Chase, 1931. (Beatrice Chase)

Sheep Shearing, from A Dartmoor Farm, Chapman & Son.

Wool prices in the 19th century were excellent in comparison with those of the 1900s when they dipped as low as threepence a pound. In Sylvester Mann's day, however, if the price was too low then the wools stayed in the barn until the following year. John Hannaford's record shows that between 1864 and 1871 the wool price dropped 50 per cent in value and that the wool appears to have been kept in the barn during the years 1867 and 1876. The longhouse, the room over the porch, was used as the wool store.

The pedigree of the ram was important. In 1902 at Widecombe Fair (originally a sheep fair) Henry Herbert Hannaford sold 20 sheep at 38 shillings and 10 at 39 shillings, earning him a return of £57.10s. Commission was 19 shillings, making his take-home return £56.11s. He purchased one ram from Mr J. Mann for £3.15s. and another from Mr Coaker for £1.17s.6d. A separate account shows his following purchases:

1901 Ram bred by R. Coaker, Sherberton
1902 Ram bred by A. Caunter, Hexworthy and ram bred by R. Coaker, Sherberton
1903 Ram bred by Mrs Wilcocks and ram bred by R. Coaker, Sherberton
1904 Ram bred by Messrs Lambshead Honywill and Wilcocks' ram.
1905 Ram bred by Mr Rowse, sire by J. Hannaford, Headland, ram bred by Mr Pethybridge of Manaton and Langdon's ram.

By law sheep had to be dipped annually to counteract the effects of diseases and parasites and there were three dips in the parish, one of which belonged to Southcombe. In 1907 the diary records:

August 23rd:
H.H.H dipping and parting sheep etc.
Mr R. Coaker here and dipped 280 sheep.
Mr W.J. Mann here dipped 367 sheep.
P.C. Collings here with dipping returns.
8 of Messrs O.Mann's and 1 of Mr J.H. French's dipped with Coaker's.

August 24th:
H.H.H dipping and parting sheep etc.
Sam looking for and parting sheep.
Mr J. Mann dipped 143 sheep.
Mr J.H. Hannaford dipped 152 sheep.

August 26th:
Mr W. Mann dipped 118 sheep.
Mr Oliver Mann dipped 131 sheep and paid.

1911
July 21st:
H.H.H dipping sheep and cutting weed.

Mr G.H. French dipped 120 sheep at 5/6 and 4/6 last year.
Mr W.W. Squire dipped 91 sheep at 6/10 pd and 53 done before.
Mr F. Nosworthy dipped 40 sheep at 2/- pd.
Mr J. Nosworthy dipped 35 sheep at 2/- pd.
Mr Oliver Mann dipped 19 sheep at 1/- pd.
Mr G. Tapper dipped 56 sheep at 2/9 pd.
Mr S. Courtier dipped 143 sheep at 6/10.

July 22nd:
Mr Owen Mann dipped 200 sheep at 9/6 pd.
Mr J. Nosworthy dipped 145 sheep at 7/-pd.
Messrs Hannaford dipped 142 sheep at 7/- pd.
Mr W. Hern dipped 160 sheep at 8/- pd.
Mr W.J. Warren dipped 3 sheep for nothing.

The total account for 1916 was recorded as:

July:
2643 sheep at £7.6.8. Labour 10/-, dips and redding £2.5.0, for wear and tear £4.11.8

August:
1344 sheep at £3.11.11. Labour 7/6, dip and redding £1.2.0, for wear and tear £2.2.5.

Sept and Oct:
2830 sheep at £7.11.1. Labour £1.12.6, dip and redding £2.14.3, for wear and tear £3.4.4.
6817 at £18.9.9. Labour £2.10.0, dip and redding £6.1.3, for wear and tear £9.18.5 less £1 for 2 crooks and iron hurdle broken £8.18.5.

Jack Prowse remembers watching the sheep being dipped at Southcombe:

The dipping trough area was surrounded by metal railings. John Hannaford used to stand on the outside of the railings with his watch in one hand and a large stick in the other. The law laid down each sheep a certain length of time. John would ensure that this time was strictly enforced and would rap his stick on the railings as the signal for the men to allow the animal out of the trough.

The forge at Linchaford. (Bessie French)

Sylvester Mann.

Dawn at Mead Hill and Sylvester Mann's flock ready to be moved to the moor. The lady on the horse was passing and asked whether she could have her photograph taken. (Sylvester Mann)

Chapter 3: Key Roles for Moorland Women

🌿 Women's Land Army 🌿

The Second World War greatly affected and changed the face of Dartmoor farming, especially in the parish of Widecombe. As much home-grown food as possible needed to be produced, in order to alleviate the costs of war – both in terms of lives and sterling; the more food that could be harvested from the fields of Britain, the more ammunition and equipment could be paid for to supply the fighting men. Land which had never been cultivated suddenly came under the plough, and this land is still in use today.

Another effect on the countryside was the influx of land girls, who

Gladys Turner, Bessie French's sister, who was a land girl in North Devon where she met and married a Cornishman named Bilkey.

arrived to take up the plough left untended by men gone off to war. According to Gladys Mann, these young ladies saved the Widecombe farmer and, as Freda Wilkinson believes, made the local lads 'look sharp' as by now they had the visiting Americans to contend with. Freda recalls:

The Women's Land Army was a national service force which operated in both world wars. All of the land girls were volunteers. Those from towns with little or no knowledge of the land or of country folk were usually billeted in hostels and went out in gangs to different larger farms to do seasonal work like hoeing or harvesting. Those, rather fewer in number, who had some practical experience already, were sent to work on individual farms; sometimes as the only girl, or indeed the only employee, on a small farm, and sometimes with one or two others. I was in the latter category as, although born in London, we had a holiday cottage on a farm in Devon where I had spent my school holidays helping to milk cows, work horses, etc. So at 18, I left school, joined the W.L.A., was sent with other recruits to Seale Hayne for five weeks practical training and eventually ended up on Dartmoor – because I could ride a horse they thought I might be

useful there! I worked at Tor Royal near Princetown for a year or two but spent the last couple of years of the war working at Lizwell Farm, Widecombe, which then belonged to Mr William Whitley of Welstor, Buckland in the Moor.

There were two other land girls there then, one – Irene Lake, a farmer's daughter from East Devon, and another, older girl called Denny, from Wales. Irene and I lodged at the farm with Mr and Mrs Rice – Mr Rice was the farm manager or 'hind' as they are known in Devon. Margery Rice, their elder daughter, a little younger than us, also worked on the farm. Denny lodged with Mr and Mrs Sam Cannon at Ponsworthy Mill. Besides Mr Rice, the only man on the farm (about 350 acres) was Tom Easterbrook, who lived at Ponsworthy. His widow, Frances, lives there still.

Besides milking the 30 odd pedigree Welsh black cows by hand, we separated the milk (turning by hand) and Irene and Mrs Rice and Margery scalded the cream and made it into butter. There was a pedigree herd of Large Black pigs too; all of the sows had botanical names like Oleria and Prunus and Mr and Mrs Whitley ingeniously gave all of their pedigree livestock born in the same year different names beginning with the same letter! There was also a flock of pedigree Kerry Hill sheep, this being a 'gentleman's farm'. Most indigenous working farmers in the Widecombe area kept (non-pedigree) South Devon cattle, Whitefaced Dartmoor sheep, one or two White or Wessex Saddleback sows, poultry, a team of not very heavy cart horses (usually called Prince or Boxer or Violet or Damsel), a ride-and-drive cob and a few Dartmoor ponies which lived year round on the common.

At Lizwell, once the milking and separating were done, I went to the stable where Tom was head horseman and I the second. We had five cart-horses (one pair was Spitfire and Hurricane) and a thoroughbred that I broke in and used for riding out to see the Lizwell cattle and sheep on Wind Tor Down and Hameldown. The rest of my time was spent with the cart horses; I broke in a couple of them too and we did harrowing, rolling, raking, and turning and sweeping in hay, carting dung, roots, flatpolls, potatoes, hay and corn in their season. Mr Rice did most of the ploughing and cut the grass and corn with the International Tractor, one of only two or three tractors owned by farmers in the whole district, although Bill Miners had two or three and did contract work with them all over Dartmoor.

Towards the end of the war, Mr Whitley decided to let Lizwell to a tenant so the workforce dispersed, but he took me on at Welstor Farm where I worked till I married a Dartmoor farmer's son, Clarry Wilkinson of Babeny. Irene married another local lad, Billy Bray from Dunstone, and Margery got married to another farmer's son, Reg Norrish from Northway. Two or three land girls who'd been at Lizwell before us had also inmarried local men, one married a Caunter from Sweaton Farm and another a Miners – there was quite a rapid turnover (more so towards the end as the local lads had to look sharp when the Yanks came to Dartmoor). They used to land Piper Cub light aircraft in Lizwell's top field and man anti-aircraft guns all over the place, and a large number of men were billeted at Buckland Court. They used to come to our weekly village dances at Widecombe in the Church House (in those days it was ballroom dancing and the Lancers). A lot of the poor blighters got killed a few months later in the D-Day invasion.

I know that there were at least two other land girls in the parish towards the end of the war; one worked for Walter Irish at Lower Cator, and the other was Gladys Weymouth (Mrs Sylvester Mann of Great Dunstone), who worked for a time at Brimpts.

We had a sort of C.O. (I forget her exact designation) in Mrs Hankey, who lived at Leusdon Lodge (and was the wife of Colonel (Retd.) Hankey who was himself C.O. of Widecombe Home Guard, below). If we had any complaint about our jobs or billets or if our farmer had complaints about us, we and they had to see this rather awe-inspiring lady and in all probability would be moved to another place. The top brass of the Devon County W.L.A. were the Committee Chairman, Lady Molesworth S.L. Aubyn, the County Secretary, Miss Bastin, and the Hon. County Organiser, Miss Medley-Costin. I came to know them as, in July 1943, I went with them and three other land girls to Buckingham Palace to tea with the Queen (now the Queen Mother) and the two Princesses to mark the occasion of the fourth birthday of the W.L.A.

We were paid by the farmer for whom we worked. Besides our board and lodging we had, I think I remember it right, 35 shillings (£1.75) per week which was the regular wage for female farm workers.

Gladys Mann remembers that she had to pay the men on Sundays 32s.6d. for a week's work and that the only concession the men gave to the Sabbath was to wear a flower in their caps. When she was working the horses she only had two commands: 'whoa back'ere round' or 'Come ere'. Horses did not wear out farm implements and the farmer would pass them onto his son.

Widecombe Home Guard. (Deborah Hannaford)

🌺 The District Nurse 🌿

For centuries, ailing parishioners had to rely on local cures or seek medical help from beyond the moor. No reference has been found to a doctor living and practising within the parish, although there are many references to people being paid to look after the sick by the Overseers of the Poor. This body would also supply additional food and clothing if required.

In 1700 Dr Ball was paid £8 'for curing Dorothy French's leg and for keeping it sound from any more costs and charges.' Eventually, however, the troublesome leg got the better of him and he returned half his fee. In 1769 Withycombe poet and curate John Gerrard, finding himself to be ill, burst forth into verse with 'An epistle' to Mr Cookesley, surgeon of Ashburton. Not seeming to get any better he wrote a tale called 'The Parley and Sickness', wherein he eventually expresses his resolution after finding the medical fraternity unable to help:

> I therefore sue to Heav'ns own laws,
> DUNNING shall vindicate my cause;
> DUNNING, whose pow'rful breath
> Can the wild rage of fiends control;
> And even plant a feeling soul
> In cold relentless death.

Eventually professional assistance was to be made available within the locality, but sadly, with the growth of car ownership, it has been lost and the sick must seek help once again from beyond the moor, just as they would have to have done in Gerrard's time.

There was, in the 1920s, a Devonshire Nursing Association, made up of local affiliated groups. In the latter part of 1926 it was proposed that a local association be formed. A letter headed 'Widecombe and Leusdon District Nurse' of 27 October 1926 contains the following:

Dear Mrs Hannaford,

I believe that you have already heard of the plan for obtaining a Nurse for this district – I send you a list now of those who are being invited to become members of the Committee of the Local Association, and hope you will have time to spare for this work.

Yours sincerely
E.C.M. Cargill

Presidents	Mrs Struben, Mrs Wetherall
Hon. Treas.	Miss Godwin
Hon. Sec.	Miss Cargill

Committee	
Mrs Walter Kitson	Mrs Hall
Mrs A. French	Mrs Hankey
Mrs Lambshead	Mrs John Hannaford
Mrs Chuter	Mrs Kernick
Mrs Wood	Mrs Snow (or Miss Mann)

A further hand-written statement reads:

It is hoped in the New Year to have an experienced District Nurse, who is also a Midwife, to work in Leusdon, Widecombe and possibly Buckland parishes. [The author has a small folded card headed 'Widecombe, Leusdon and Buckland Nursing Association,' setting out the association's rules.]. The need for one in these isolated parts is more and more realised, and often her advice and help would save calling in a doctor – As many as possible are asked to become annual subscribers. The scale of charges, by the Devon Nursing Association for general nursing is:- Class 1 Labourers 4/- a year; Class II Smallholders and trades people 6/- a year; Class III Farmers 10/- a year. In each class subscription includes wives and children under 16, also unmarried and non-earning sons and daughters living at home. Unmarried wage earners under the same roof pay half subscription – Extra charges to subscribers for midwifery:- Class 1 21/-, Class II 25/-, Class III 30/-. Three months notice must be given to the Nurse and the fee prepaid or ½ the fee at the time of engagement and the balance at the confinement. The Nurse is responsible for the care of the mother and child for 10 days and longer if necessary. Night duty is not expected of the Nurse except in critical cases, when a small charge may be made, or in maternity cases, in which no additional charge is made for night duty. The Nurse's services, if not required for subscribers, may be supplied to non subscribers, but only at higher rates, from 1/- a visit General Nursing and Double fees Midwifery, and Maternity Nursing Subscriptions to be paid quarterly.

The author's grandmother, Mrs Margaret McCrea, was a collector, and the author often accompanied her on her quarterly rounds. In many cases a return visit was required if the subscriber was out or did not have the money to hand. The nurse must have been very welcome in

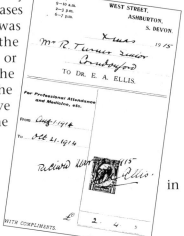

Right: *Quarterly subscription of Mr R. Turner senr of Corndonford, 1914.*
(Bessie French)

The first full annual account of the Widecombe, Leusdon and Buckland Nursing Association, 1927-28.
(Hermon French)

Widecombe, for in the second year's accounts allowance is made for a 'House and Car Fund':

Receipts	£	s.	d.
Proceeds of the Fête	189	8	11
Donations	118	8	0
Sales of work	9	7	6
	316	16	5

Expenditure	£	s.	d.
Furnishing house, etc.	63	3	7
Purchase of car, licenses, Insurance and upkeep	156	17	9
Rent of garage	2	19	0
Expenses of Fête	11	9	4
Balance March 31st 1929	80	6	9
	316	16	5

It is believed that the nurse's house was built using the subscriptions of local people on land at Higher Dunstone given by Mr William Whitley of Welstor, who then owned Great Dunstone Farm.

The commoners of Dunstone Manor noted the assistance provided by the County Council in easing the rough journey across the common to her house and garage at the Manor Court on 16 October 1959:

We present that the Devon County Council have surfaced with Tarmac the road to the Nurse's house whereas they hold a right of way only over this road. We request the Steward to write to the Clerk of the Council pointing out the positions.

Previously the nurse had garaged her car in a lean-to down on the road half way between the Lower Dunstone turn-off and Lady Meadow Terrace.

Chapter 4: Afforestation

The plantations at Brimpts were planted under the direction of Charles Barrington, Duchy Bailiff, in 1862 and were cut down by Portuguese labourers during the First World War (although they have since been replanted). The Portuguese were referred to by the locals as 'prisoners of war' and they lived in wooden huts dotted around the area, one of which survives on the banks of the Dart at Huccaby. Their trunks were transported to the railhead at Princetown on an overhead ropeway suspended from wooden towers. One of these structures is said to have been used to weigh horses at Huccaby Races (*right*).

In 1930 the Forestry Commission began planting Bellever and Laughter Hole newtakes and in 1945 the Commission was cultivating Soussons Down – originally a small rabbit warren. The name Soussons is thought to be

the colloquial corruption of South (tin) Sands. The lodes of tin ore run east-west on Dartmoor. The Redwater flows south through these veins and over the millennia the largest pebbles were deposited first and finally at the lower end, the finest deposits being spread out over the entire width of the valley. The tinner working his way up river came upon these deposits first then, higher up the valley, found larger tin stones which revealed the proximity of the original veins and opencast workings reaching out from the east and west. Miners then sought the ore from shafts and adits. Here then was an industrial complex that could support an enterprising worker and his family.

Freda Wilkinson remembers:

When Clarry and I married, he took a job as a forestry worker on Bellever Forest at £3 per week and we were able to rent the 'Forest Worker's Holding' at Laughter Hole, a three-bedroomed bungalow and 17½ acres for 5 shillings (25 pence) per week. After a year he got added proficiency pay of 5 shillings per week and sometimes used our own horse for pulling out timber which brought us in another 10 shillings a day. In 1947 the Forestry Commission bought Soussons Down from the Duchy, which had been largely a rabbit-warren like headland. They also acquired an ex-U.S. Army track-laying tractor and a 'prairie-buster' plough with which Clarry ploughed furrows about 2½ feet deep at intervals of about 3 feet

---

WIDECOMBE, ASHBURTON, and TORBRYAN, DEVON.

To Timber Merchants, Mine Agents, Contractors and Others.

Important Sale of Prime Oak, Ash, Larch, Elm, and other Timber.

Messrs.

SAWDYE & SON

are instructed by the different Owners

TO SELL BY AUCTION,

AT THE GOLDEN LION HOTEL, ASHBURTON,

on Thursday, 24th of February, 1898,

at 3 o'clock in the Afternoon,

327 Oak, 103 Ash, 414 Larch, 7 Elm, 5 Beech and 1 Scotch

TIMBER TREES,

with their Tops, Lops, and Bark,

now standing on LINCHAFORD, WATERLEAT and BREMRIDGE Estates, in the respective Parishes of Widecombe, Ashburton, and Torbryan, and numerically marked with White Paint.

[over!]

Left: *Notice for an auction of timber, 1898.* (Geoff Weymouth)

445

White Slade or Snaily House on East Dart, looking down the river. Sept 2 1893

Images by Robert Burnard of Snaily House (top) and Bellaford Farm looking east, 1889. Bellaford is known today as Bellever.

The last of the wood and iron huts built for the Portuguese internees during the First World War.

all over the Soussons Down. *The furrows were turned over onto the unploughed strip of ground to make twice the depth of soil to plant the young Sitka spruce on, leaving gutters in between for drainage. Redvers Webb from Postbridge [a one-time tin-miner like several of the forest workers), used to walk behind the plough, partly to make sure that the furrows turned over properly and partly to run for help if Clarry and the tractor and plough disappeared down a hidden mine shaft or into an unplumbed bog.*

Archaeologists also followed the plough like seagulls, looking for flints and things, Hansford Worth amongst them. [The author's brother also searched the furrows finding, among other things, a beautiful single-tanged arrowhead and a small bronze ingot.]. *Clarry got paid extra for that work too, so we were in the money!*

Farmer's sons who worked at home in those days did not get paid and had to get their pocket money by catching and selling rabbits in their spare time. Farmer's daughters working at home rarely had even that opportunity. When Sylvester Mann was a boy there were three ways of earning pocket money; catching rabbits, catching moles and selling honey. He remembered when a local poacher was fined ten bob by the magistrate and caught sufficient rabbits on the way back from court to pay the fine! Moles get regular recordings in the Southcombe diaries: on 26 January1903, J. Leaman had 18 mole traps and on 6 April had 77 mole tails. The same year Henry Herbert Hannaford paid Mr Dueel 4s.5d. for 28 moles. He also says that the mole skins would be nailed out on the barn door to cure.

Sylvester also made money from honey; but upon being asked how he came by the bees he simply said that he caught them – a swarm settled in a local tree, he knocked them off into a box, made a hive (*right*), and was in business.

On Linchaford, Widecombe-in-the Moor.

Lot				
1.	17 OAK TREES, numbered	1 to 17,	both inclusive
„ 2.	18 ditto	„	18 to 35,	„
„ 3.	20 ditto	„	36 to 55,	„
„ 4.	18 ditto	„	57 to 74,	„
„ 5.	12 ASH TREES,	„	1 to 12,	„
„ 6.	8 ditto	„	13 to 20,	„
„ 7.	4 ditto	„	21 to 24,	„
„ 8.	50 LARCH TREES,	„	1	
„ 9.	73 ditto	„	2	
„ 10.	54 ditto	„	3	
„ 11.	50 ditto	„	4	
„ 12.	61 ditto	„	5	
„ 13.	41 ditto	„	6	
„ 14.	43 ditto	„	7	
„ 15.	42 ditto	„	8.	

Waterleat Wood (and Lands adjoining), Ashburton.

Lot				
16.	12 OAK TREES, numbered	1 to 12,	both inclusive
„ 17.	14 ditto	„	13 to 26,	„
„ 18.	17 ditto	„	27 to 43,	„
„ 19.	18 ditto	„	44 to 61,	„
„ 20.	5 ASH TREES	„	1 to 5	„

On Bremridge, Torbryan.

Lot				
21.	40 OAK TREES, numbered	1 to 40,	both inclusive
„ 22	40 ditto	„	41 to 80,	„
„ 23.	40 ditto	„	81 to 120,	„
„ 24.	35 ditto	„	121 to 155,	„
„ 25.	21 ditto	„	156 to 176,	„
„ 26.	17 ditto	„	177 to 193.	„

On Bremridge, Torbryan *(continued)*.

Lot				
27.	11 ASH TREES, numbered	1 to 11,	both inclusive
„ 28.	12 ditto	„	12 to 23,	„
„ 29.	21 ditto	„	24 to 44,	„
„ 30.	18 ditto	„	45 to 62,	„
„ 31.	12 ditto	„	63 to 74,	„
„ 32.	7 ELM TREES	„	1 to 7,	„
„ 33.	5 BEECH and 1 SCOTCH numbered 1 to 5 and 1 respectively.			

The above Timber is deserving of especial attention, most of the Oak is of long lengths, good size, hearty, with plenty of Bark and Tops ; the Ash is clean and tough, the Lot at Widecombe being also of large size ; the Larch is very prime, being straight grown, long lengths and very hearty. The other Lots are of a most useful description, and the whole stands well for removal being near good roads.

☞ To VIEW the different Lots application should be made to Mr. W. MANN at Ponsworthy, Mr. STANBURY at Bremridge, and the AUCTIONEERS at Ashburton, who will have a person to show the Lots on any Monday or Thursday previous to the Sale, between the hours of 10 a.m. and 3 p.m.

Refreshments will be provided at the Golden Lion Hotel, at 2 p.m., at 2/ each returnable to Purchasers.

General Auction, Agency, Surveyingand Insurance Offices, Ashburton. Feb. 3rd, 1898.

C. N. DENT, Printer, Ashburton.

Notice of timber auction on 3 February 1898.

The well which provides the water for Lower Dunstone Farm.

The one-time water supply for Stouts Cottages beside the road to Natsworthy.

Chapter 5: Water

Writing in 1901, William Crossing made the comment that:

The beneficial climatic influence of Dartmoor over the county of Devon cannot be over-estimated. The Moor acts as a huge sponge, storing up the rainfall, and pouring it liberally, by means of the numerous streams, on every hand.

For 'every hand' we might substitute 'every greedy hand,' for the envious eyes of the low-landers were long cast in the direction of this natural abundance to quench their ever-growing thirst. The waters of five major reservoirs now cover once attractive valleys, and much of our heritage lies submerged below their surface. The author wonders if Crossing thought seriously about the implications of his statement, for the subject seems to bring out acrimony and contention on all sides.

The commonest granite utensil is the trough, and they abound on every farmstead whether filled or in ruins, and can even be found on the open moor. They come in all shapes and sizes, some are very rough and ready, others with a fine finish. It is impossible to date troughs but many may have been in use for centuries, ever since the farmstead was first occupied and water required for drinking. In the main they started life as the household dipping trough, later to become the feeding trough for livestock.

Those proceeding up the Natsworthy road from Widecombe will probably be unaware of the fact that the small trough beside the road above Stouts Cottages and about 20 feet below the 'J Moil' stone opposite was the water supply for these cottages (referred to in 1475 as 'lands called Stodfoldi's in demesne of Notysworthe').

Violet Warren said that in her youth she scrubbed this trough clean every week because it supplied clean water, although they would go further afield for drinking water. Many dwellings had wells, some being updated with a hand pump. If these had to be dug to any depth it was the tinner, an expert in water works, who would be called in to perform the task. The Dymonds recorded

Lily Kernick and Louie and Andrew Harvey, c.1910, drawing water from the village well. (May Hambley)

this long operation on Monday 17 October 1870:

... the chief event being the opening of the Well which was found to be sunk about 20 feet through softish granite – at the bottom about a foot of dirty water over a deposit of sand fallen in from the sides.

On the following day we have:

The miner had been very busy all day about the Well. After all the water had been brought up in a bucket the miner was let down in a sort of bucket and by degrees sent up the dirt and then after a time pieces of granite he had knocked off. He drilled into the rock and water has begun to come already tho they have not blasted at all as yet.

On 19 October:

Cornick the Cornish miner was at work most of the day – several attempts at blasting were unsuccessful – the water coming in too rapidly – but in the afternoon after much preparation there was a slight rumble – and the result appeared to be satisfactory to the minds of the chief actors.

Finally, two days later, we are told that:

This afternoon we had the pleasure of tasting a beautiful glass of cold water brought up from the depths of the well, the sinking of which has proved a much less troublesome job than was expected.

Nearly 120 years later in 1989 the late Mr John Gooch of Sheena Towers sought to improve his water supply by looking for water on his own land. He contacted an authority who suggested he employ a diviner. Mr Gooch watched the diviner's performance with great interest; first he surveyed the site with a pair of steel rods, the ends of which seemed to come together at a certain spot, the diviner then took a traditional hazel twig concentrating on the area indicated and not only did the twig arch upwards but the diviner did as well! Water was found on this spot 20 feet down.

A hard drill was brought in and a 6-inch bore driven 42 feet. On the following day a 4-inch

The fishpond on Dockwell and (inset) the pond in the making.

bore was sunk 200 feet. It was not just water that was found, but China clay and no granite to obstruct the work.

Whether because of the water pressure or the force of the drill, a mixture of water and china clay shot up into the sky and deluged the surrounding area with a thick solution of white muck. The land hereabouts has been the home of the mole for centuries and the solution leaked into their tunnels and exuded out all over the garden. The drilling gear was removed, a pump installed and some 6000 gallons of water run off, leaving, when tested, an excellent supply of pure water fit to quench the thirst of any weary traveller.

Villages also had public supplies; the one in Widecombe is often described as Saxon although there is no real evidence to support this claim. Here the water is piped to the well from a spring in the garden behind and it has never been known to run dry. In times of drought, however, it is kept locked and those who need it have a key for their personal benefit.

The author has a letter from Mr F. Bucholson dated 19 November 1901, to Baron De Hochepied of Wooder Manor, in which, under the heading 'South Devon Water', he describes visiting the site and proposes a scheme to impound water covering a 40-acre area to hold 11 000 000 gallons for each foot of depth. By building a dam across the valley it would, he argues, be possible to increase the amount to 4½ million gallons per foot of depth, sufficient to supply half of Teignmouth's demand. The water would be taken by 9-inch pipe to Holne Bridge and then on to the Teignmouth

Reservoir, with any surplus possibly being sold to neighbouring towns. Mr Bucholson also gave consideration to driving an electrical turbine, as the water would fall some 60 feet, to supply electricity to the surrounding area. He considered Cockingford Mill, noting:

I should suggest that by you putting in a turbine at the Mill or a water wheel of better efficiency, all objections in this quarter might easily be overcome.

The scheme did not go ahead and Teignmouth sought its water at Fernworthy.

Top: *Old pump set above a well at the Mill, Widecombe.*
Above: *A 1911 photograph of the old well by Chapman & Son.* (Ena Prowse)

Julia Hambley walking to the village during the ammil of 1946/7. (Julia Morley née Hambley)

F. and B. Learie with Mrs West at the ford over Wallabrook at Babeny, 1891. (Robert Burnard)

Chapter 6: Weathering the Storm

The winter of 1946/7 was to go out with a bang. It was not just cold with heavy falls of snow, but it brought with it an ammil (*opposite*), the phenomenon of rain which turns to ice wherever it lies. Sylvia Needham remembers it well; she weighed a small twig coated with ice and the scales settled at 14½ oz although they would not register the weight of the twig when defrosted. What stuck in her mind was the bang as great boughs finally succumbed to the weight of ice and either fractured or broke off, a sound that at times was almost continuous.

Dorothy Williams remembers it too, for her mother lived at Huccaby Tor Cottage known as Mazedman (or Meresman) Cottage and she fell ill. Dorothy and her husband tried to drive out but only got as far as Ollsbrim, snow preventing them going any further. They went on foot down Yar Tor Hill and up the other side in an attempt to overcome this and when they even-tually returned someone had written 'You silly B's' in the snow beside their car! Dorothy also remembered that in the great freeze of 1963 her mother was again taken ill and a doctor came out by helicopter and landed in the field opposite the cottage.

Hermon French recorded the great snow of 1946/7 day by day. The following comprises a few extracts from his diary:

Jan 28: Trying to thaw pipes which are all frozen. Shall have to shift bullocks to Meadow in morning, parted a fresh piece of cabbage for sheep.

Jan 29: No.3 lamb arrived, intermittent snow and very severe frost. Put horses in Meadow and Chapel Moor, and put bullocks in Higher Meadow and Long Close because all other water is frozen. Min 10°F – Max 25°F. Wind NE. 6" snow.

Jan 30: Striving to feed cattle and sheep and poultry in blizzard. Min 10°F – 25°F. 2" snow... frost in dining room 9 p.m. Fire going.

Jan 31: No.4 lamb born dead No. 5 & 6 twins all right. Cut paths to both hayricks and also dung heap. Snow stopped falling this morning.

Feb 2: Blizzard all last night turning to rain. Gale SE turning W, much devastation to trees in garden.

Feb 5: Heavily overcast, intermittent snow p.m. Made wide runner sleigh for use in soft snow, perfect snow crystals of many patterns fell today.

Feb 8: No 13 & 14 lambs arrived, a double: continuous snow a.m. 12 ewes have lambed and 12 lambs are living. 1 ewe without lambs and 1 ewe dead. 10 ewes with 12 lambs. J. Williams called tonight for a shovel and lantern to get his tractor out of a snow drift. Slight thaw today with fog freezing in to bushes.

Feb 11: Cleared out fowls' loft and made a bit more room for fowls to feed, very cold freezing continuously with ice fog: bushes, etc. have a blade of ice ³⁄₄" wide on every twig: the blade is edge on to the east, no ice on lee-side of twig nor anywhere on shelter side of hedges.

Feb 12: During last night a fringe of needle-like crystals has grown on to the ice and is still growing today; in exposed places the combined growth of ice and crystal fringe is 1½" to 1³⁄₄" wide. All on the windward side of each twig: thorns and other thick bushes are now quite opaque.

Feb 15: Claude borrowed my sleigh. Saw a starving fox this evening barking as it trotted around. Frost day and night.

Feb 20: Still severe frost day and night. Slight continuous snow falling all day, barometer falling rapidly. Put a lot of bags of straw in potato house to stop draught. Blizzard started about 6 p.m. took acetylene lamp to Square Park and dug and heaped 3 days' supply of cabbage.

Feb 21: About 6" snow drifting to 2 ft or more on top of old snow and in exactly same drifts and position.

Feb 22: Continuous snow. Strong volume of sound from South.

Mar 4: 2" of snow between 8 and 10 p.m. and all day today intermittent freezing rain. There is now a sheet of clear ice ½" thick on everything. Robertson brought 3 cwt coal and got stuck and can't get away again.

Mar 5: There is now from 1" to 2" clear ice on everything after heavy continuous freezing rain. Widespread damage to trees and bushes but reports say nothing below Poundsgate. A NE blizzard commencing tonight 3" snow by 8 p.m.

Mar 9: Aurora tonight. 1 ewe died, brought in

Clearing the moorland road. (Julia Morley)

Dockwell, 1947. (Hermon French Collection)

Jack Brown and his wife outside their home now known as Tremills, Lower Dunstone. (Phyllis Pascoe)

The Bearas. (Eileen Exell and Dorothy Williams)

The road to Venton at Sentry Hill. The field on the right, below the churchyard, was called Sanctuary before being corrupted to Sentry. (Julia Morley)

❧ Winter 1962/3 ❧

Below: *Bill Fursdon of Oldwalls, 1962.* (Liz Fursdon)

Above: *Natsworthy driveway in January 1963.* (Deborah Hannaford)

Below: *Philip and Susan Hannaford at Natsworthy Gate, January 1963.* (Deborah Hannaford)

Above: *Jordan Lane, 1962.* (Liz Fursdon)

The School, Widecombe-in-the-Moor.

Widecombe Hill is a bitter pill
For those who have to climb it.
But a guide from the top for a good teashop
Stop at the North Hall behind it.

Main picture: *One of the small photographs which Mary Willcocks sold with poems (written, it is thought, by herself) at the North Hall Café which she ran for many years and which stood beside the Natsworthy road close to the site of the original North Hall/Widecombe Town Manor.* (Geoff Weymouth)
Inset: *The café was demolished overnight during the great freeze of 1963 when it collapsed under the weight of the ice and snow. It had been built by Tom Nosworthy.*

lamb, then by 1.30 p.m. the leading edge of a SE blizzard reached us without any warning.

Mar 13: Cleared out calves' house: let out fowls for the first time since Jan 29th, 2 lambs died in great rain storm which lasted all night. 12 lambs left alive out of 19, 14 ewes out of 16 left alive. Thaw continues. Started digging pit to bury dead sheep and lambs.

March 22: Last of snow on the farm probably melted today.

Freda Wilkinson's story surrounding the same dramatic spell of weather embodies a wonderful tribute to Dartmoor people:

Those of us whose memory stretches back half a century will all remember the great freeze of February and March 1947. The war was over but food was still rationed, as were petrol, animal feed-stuffs and many other necessities of life.

We, that is my husband, myself, and our three-month-old baby son lived at Laughter Hole Farm, a forest worker's holding of 17½ acres, in the middle of Dartmoor, at a 1000-ft elevation, and 1 mile from the nearest neighbour (the nearby Laughter Hole House being only occupied in holiday times).

We had no telephone, no electricity of course, and we pumped out water by hand from a well under the back kitchen floor.

My husband's parents, brother and sister farmed Babeny, a Duchy farm a couple of miles away across the East Dart river (but about 5 miles away by car). My sister and her family lived about 3 miles away, near Postbridge, and we had neighbours at

Dunnabridge and at Brimpts, both about 2 miles away across country, and several others at Bellever, only a mile down the road through the plantations.

Besides ourselves and a couple of dogs and cats, we had farm animals to feed, a cart cob, two riding ponies, a few Dartmoor ponies, a score of Devon Closewool ewes, 5 South Devon cows and heifers, some calves and a dozen Light Sussex hens. Fortunately we had the use of father-in-law's 40-acre newtake on our side of the river for rough grazing – gorse and heather being more use in the winter than grass – but almost all the winter fodder, hay, potatoes, swedes and oats, had been produced on our own few small fields. We were probably the last to mow oats with a scythe and bind the sheaves by hand as it wasn't worth any contractor's while to bring a binder miles out into the wilds to cut an acre of corn.

So, that was the scene at the end of January 1947. By the 23rd Jan. according to my diary, the wind was in the east and very, very cold. By the 25th. the snow started to fall. C. (my husband) had just finished steeping (laying) the meadow hedge and we carted in a load of hay from the hayrick to the barn. The next day it was snowing too hard to leave the cows out, they came back into the shippon after they'd drunk at the little spring-fed pond in the yard. For a couple more days wheeled vehicles were still able to get about, we had ½ a ton of coal delivered by Bolts' of Princetown, and C. and his brother got a tractor-drawn trailer load of straw over to us from Babeny. On Wednesday 29th Jan C. went to Newton Abbot, walking to Ponsworthy and then in Ronnie Hill's cattle lorry. He brought 2 heifer calves

(£4.12s. and £4) but Ronnie's lorry broke down and Bill Miners from Widecombe brought them back to Babeny; he couldn't get to Laughter for the snow. So C. and his brother brought the calves (hardly a week old), carrying them most of the way, up through the snow drifts onto the open moor of Riddon Ridge, then down to the river across the stepping stones – great ice- glazed boulders a yard or more apart – and up the last half mile through the plantations to home where we gave them warm milk and Vitalis. They survived – the men too, though they probably had some-thing stronger to drink.

Heavy snow fell all that night, driven by a merciless east wind, and by the next day snow drifts had made the roads impassable. Bolts' of Princetown had always delivered groceries, bread, meat and fuel to the outlying settlements, and no one could have tried harder than they to reach their customers, but it was some days before the main road from Princetown to Postbridge was cleared enough for anything to get through. Most of the snow clearance that winter was done by hand, neighbours helping each other and the road-men to shovel a way through the drifts, which usually filled the road in again within a few hours.

In those days we all stored food for the Winter – most farming families had killed and salted down a pig before Christmas. We had big jars of salted string beans, buckets of eggs in water-glass, and potatoes and swedes in caves or clamps. In our case we had enough milk from our own cows, though of course the calves had most of it, so there wasn't enough at that time of year to make cream or butter. Then there were the rabbits, very plentiful at that time, before myxomatosis had been heard of, and easy to 'trace' in the snow and catch with ferret and nets. We had them stewed, fried, baked and made into pies, and nailed their skins up inside the wood shed doors. The dogs and cats shared them with us. I remember our spaniel, Flicka, coming home one day after paddling through part of the river, with her tail and her 'trousers' weighted down with balls of ice the size of oranges.

On Feb 1st there was a terrific snowstorm in the night and the drifts were higher than ever. Our house had the Forestry plantations to the west and north but no shelter at all from the cruel east wind. The windows, most of which faced east, were coat-ed outside with blown snow and ice for at least six weeks, and when we woke in the mornings, in bed with the baby between us for warmth, the coverlet was crusted with ice from our breath frozen during the night. Our baby wasn't able to go outside the

house for weeks, but the solid fuel stove kept the living-room warm, and besides our coal supply we had plenty of wood, mainly from a big dead sycamore, just inside the plantation above the barn, that had been ring-barked by the Forestry. C. felled it with his axe – no chainsaws in those days – and we sawed it up and split the logs – two warmings from that wood, as they say!

I milked the cows and fed the calves and other livestock but could not of course leave the farm until it was safe to take the baby out. C. spent his days trudging and clambering through the drifts to Postbridge for food; to Bellever to help the other Forestry men dig through the drifts; and to Babeny. His sister and their neighbour Ruby, from Sherril, rode their ponies, hoofs well packed with grease to stop the snow forming ice-balls under their feet, up to Ollsbrim, 3 miles there and back, to collect bread and groceries that had, sometimes, been left there for them. It was 7 weeks before the Sherril Hill road was opened to traffic.

Eileen Willcocks, 1928. It is hard to believe that she was just recovering from diphtheria. (Eileen Exell and Dorothy Williams)

On the 2nd and 3rd of February it thawed a bit and we had rain instead of snow, though on the 4th there was still at least a foot of snow even where there were no drifts and there were drifts up against every wall and hedge and in every road. On the 5th brother-in-law came over to help get in a couple of cart loads of hay. It had to be cut out from the rick in blocks with a hay-knife and then loaded on to a wain and unloaded into the tallet or the barn. The meadow gateway was iced up and Blackie, the cart horse, slipped and fell whilst bringing in the second load. Fortunately he only grazed his knees but we didn't dare try that again, so for the next 5 or 6 weeks all the hay had to be carried in from the hayrick on our backs. The next day C. spent help-ing get in hay at Babeny but they had a tractor so, although they had difficulties with that, they were not the same.

That day my sister and her husband walked the 3 miles from their place with tea and biscuits and cigarettes and a food parcel from our other sister in America – what a bonanza! They had left their two little boys, aged 4 and 8, with Mrs Williams the forester's wife, at Bellever, as the little chaps were tired out by the time they got there. My brother-in-law, who was a teacher at Sutton High in Plymouth, had about 8 weeks off that term, as it was impossi-ble to get to Plymouth from Postbridge in his car. Their older son had 6 weeks' holiday from Princetown Primary too – 3 weeks because the road was impassable and 3 because the school lavatories were out of action because of the frost.

There was more snow the next day and C. spent the following 2 days helping shovel through the drifts between Bellever and Postbridge. On the 10th Feb C. set off for Princetown on Blackie to get provisions, as we were running out of essentials. By that time the drifts that covered the walls and gates were frozen so hard that he was able to lead the horse over the walls and over the wires, they went straight as a line to Bolts' shop – it would have been about 5 miles by road and through the gates but was nearer 3 the way they went. He led Blackie back with the saddle loaded up on each side and on top like a pack-saddle with our groceries and bread, and bread for Mrs Williams and Mrs Bray at Bellever.

On the 12th C. and his brother managed to get to Newton Abbot by motorbike and fetch back groceries for their mother. On the 13th C. went to Brimpts to help old Mr Down and his daughter cart in hay. On the 14th our neighbours from Bellever, Mr and Mrs Bray, battled up on foot in the evening with bread and to see how the baby and I were. Fortunately our little son, who had come home from the nursing home where he was born weighing only 5¾lbs, having suffered from pyloric stenosis during his first week of life, was gaining weight satisfactorily, now being 12½ lbs, and at the end of the month 14½ lbs. It was lucky I was feeding him myself and he was having the government ration of cod liver oil and a little Virol as well. He never had a sniffle all through that dreadful winter, possibly because there was no one but his parents to catch germs from or perhaps it was too cold for any germs to get about.

My four-year-old nephew in Postbridge was poorly for a few days during that time and the younger of the two doctors in Chagford rode a horse out to Postbridge to see him and other patients out there.

There was more heavy snow on the 21st Feb and C. walked the 3 miles to my sister's for a loaf as Bolts' had managed to get out to Postbridge a couple of days before. My sister had a telephone but it was of no use, all the wires were down. But Miss Bolt used to decide what her customers would need, knowing their preferences and what size their families were, and she saw that they got what they needed if it was humanly possible. On the next day, the 22nd, C. and Mr Bray walked to Bolts' and back for the week's groceries and bread.

The following day we lost a Dartmoor mare, she had a dead foal in her and died of septicemia – no antibiotics available then. The Dartmoor ponies were having oaten straw to supplement the gorse they were nibbling off the taller bushes in the newtake. Gorse, or furze as we call it, is very nutritious even in the winter, the ponies pound it with their hooves to crush the spines, and in earlier times Dartmoor farmers used to cut it and pound it to enable their cattle to eat it in the winter: 'Ye bruise the furze without delay – to keep the cows alive till

May' was an old saying. Our cows were having a few swedes as well as their hay and the sheep had swedes thrown out to them from the cave and a little hay.

The poultry lived on boiled 'tetties' and household scraps and what oats the horses wasted. At this time Peter Hannaford at Sherril was using his old 'drashel' (flail) to thresh out a bit of dredge corn (oats and barley mixed) from the sheaf for his fowls.

On the 23rd C. went to Powder Mills with the Caunters from Dunnabridge; some ponies had been got in there from the high northern moor. Some of theirs were there and C. helped to drive them home. On the 27th our ewes started lambing and though the ewes looked in reasonably good condition the lack of normal nourishment and exercise had affected the unborn lambs and several were born dead or died the same day despite all we could do for them. Fortunately we didn't lose any ewes.

On the 4th March we had rain in the evening which froze as it pitched and the following morning every twig was encased in ice an inch thick, as was the lying snow and the drifts and everything on which the rain had landed – 'ammil', as the glazed frost is known on Dartmoor; beautiful but deadly. Wild birds lay frozen to death where they had dropped, and most of the branches on the east side of the trees had come crashing down to the ground with their weight of ice. By the 9th March the wind turned and the thaw began, rain melting the snow and disclosing the land again and, over across the river on the open moor, sad remains of Scotch sheep and even Dartmoor ponies that had been under the drifts. The foxes and crows and ravens soon found them. We were lucky that we had so few animals to support and that we were young and strong, but some of the farmers who had large flocks of Scotch sheep and traditional herds of ponies 'learing' on the wilder parts of the Moor away from the farmsteads lost a lot of the stock.

We had a little more snow on the 14th and 15th of March. On the 15th we had some visitors from Tavistock who walked up to our place from Bellever where they'd left their car stuck in a snow drift. C. went down with a shovel to help dig it out. But spring was on its way, the cows could go out by day, the young bullocks kicked their heels and gambolled in the sunshine, the lambs that had survived were jumping to play, the hens were getting redheaded, and I was able to carry the baby out to see his neighbours and relations. In some ways our little community, scattered though it was, was better able to cope than would be the case today when we are so reliant on electricity – that would have broken down [as would have] telephones, mains water (the pipes would have frozen) and things like convenience foods and disposable nappies, which were unheard of then. And we all helped each other, as was the custom in those days.

Little Meadow. (Suzanne Hutchins)

Ten years before that treacherous winter of 1946/7, Widecombe found itself in the grip of a far more brief, but no less ferocious, battering dealt out by Mother Nature. On the night of 4 August 1938, Corndonford found itself in the thick of a storm which Hermon and Edith French (*left*) watched with awe:

Lightning struck at Dockwell in the pond – breaking off an ash branch from bushes on the bank – and was believed to have been seen from Watergate where it seemed to curve in towards the house.

Another lightning strike, seen from windows here, seemed to be a foot wide. It struck upwards from the ground to cloud through the lower hedge of Crowdy Park, scorching the Sycamore bushes growing on the spot. The lightning also scorched the outer ring of leaves of the sheep's sorrel plants growing within a radius of 20-30 feet. The side of the higher hedge of Square Park [was struck] ripping out a strip of turf two feet wide and scattering it over an area 20 yards in diameter

The row of potatoes growing at the foot of the hedge was cut across and the potatoes laid bare and cooked. A week or two after, the bracken on Corndon was turned brown in circular patches scattered all over the hillside as seen from Dockwell. Five and a half inches of rain fell in three hours.

Chapter 7: The Parish and Its Manor Bounds

In order to grasp the layout and extent of the parish bounds of Widecombe, one will do better to look at those of the seven manors within it, for historically, the parish included the Ancient Tenements, the areas of which have long been undefined and which therefore make it impossible to calculate an exact outline.

The manors of Widecombe parish include Dunstone and Blackslade, Widecombe Town Manor or North Hall, Natsworthy, Blackaton (previously known as Blagdon Pippard), Jordan (previously known as Dewdon) and Spitchwick. The author has not seen the bounds of Dewdon set down on paper and when it became known as Jordan or at what point in time is unclear. The same mystery surrounds the renaming of Blagdon Pippard. Whereas Wilfred Jones, who owned Blackaton Manor, stated that his records only went back 30 years, John Stone of Lower Blackaton Farm said that his documentation dates back to 1922 when a Robert Fleming conveyed to John Willcock 'all that Manor or Reputed Manor and Lordship of Blackaton known by the several names of Lower Blackaton Farm, Upper Blackaton Farm and Blackaton Downs Farm.'

Left: *Chart of the late 1800s showing calculated acreages of Widecombe's manors, woods, roads, rivers and commons.*

Below: *Photograph by Chapman & Son of the Rugglestone.* (Suzanne Hutchins)

Collecting 'chief rents' at the Dun Stone, Lower Dunstone. (Dymond Diaries)

Beating the bounds of Dunstone and Blackslade – outside the Rugglestone Inn, 1963.
Left to right: Geoffrey Michelmore (agent), Tim Reep (Chittleford),
Raymond Warren (Lower Dunstone), Audrey Lamb (Rugglestone Inn), Peter Hicks (Venton),
John Horton (Tunhill), Andrew Horton, Mary Hamlyn (Dunstone Manor). (Iris Woods)

❧ Dunstone and Blackslade ❧

A part of Widecombe parish since Ralph de Pomeroy received them as recorded in the Domesday Book, Dunstone and Blackslade were bought in 1784 by William Norrish from the Hamlyns. In 1869, Robert Dymond took them over and they have remained in his family ever since.

On 31 May 1985 Marianne Margaret Hamlyn (known as Mary) was laid to rest among her ancestors in Widecombe churchyard. With her death (at the age of 84) there ended over 750 years of continuous connection between the Hamlyn family and the parish

Above: *Seven Lords Land and Cairn Circle.*

of Widecombe-in-the-Moor – and, possibly, with one of the farms that made up the manor of Dunstone. Mary could trace her bloodline back to Richard Hamlyn of Larkbeare, father of two sons, Henry Hamlyn of Larkbeare, Dunstone and Runnage in Widecombe, and William Hamlyn of Hill in Holne (Fines 1219, Assye Roll 1238). The name Hamlyn has appeared in a multitude of forms over the years, including Hamlin, Hamley, Hamling(e), Hamelyne and, before 1258, Hamelin. A Hamelin crossed the Channel with William of Normandy and was one of the Count of Mortain's men, whose family tree can be traced to the first Duke of Cornwall and on down to Charles, Prince of Wales.

According to an inquisition in 1556, Robert Hamlyn states that at the end of his life he was:

... seised in fee of five messuages, five barns, five

gardens, 150 acres of land, 20 acres of meadow, 100 acres of fize and heath in Chytelford, Scobtorr, Fenton, Dunston and Blaxslade within the parish of Wydecombe.

In fact, the name Hamlyn crops up in relation to the ownership or occupancy of many of the farms of Widecombe Parish. These include: Dunstone, Chittleford, Blackslade, Scobitor, Venton, Southway, Wooder, Southcombe, East Shallowfield, Lower and Higher Hannaford, Lower and Higher Aish, Uppercot and Lake. Thomas Hamlyn rebuilt Lake, putting his initials and date 'T.H.1661' over the door, and the family stayed there until 1958.

Robert Dymond held court in 1872 and in the 1877 court confirmed the bounds of the joint manors of Dunstone and Blackslade as:

Commencing at Rugglestone, passing by nearly a straight line at the back of the roadside Inn now occupied by James Lee to Hindsfoot or Hennafoot stone in Rugglestone Moor; and from thence in a Southerly direction to the point where the water from Southcombe Well joins the River Wittern or Webburn; from thence following the course of the said water to its source at Southcombe well; from thence in a straight line to Two Crosses, and from thence in a straight line to the west point of a heap of rocks called Wind Tor; and from thence to the higher corner of a field part of Higher Dunstone

Kingshead, 1947. (Sir William Van Straubenzee)

Lower Dunstone, the site of a Saxon settlement.

Above left: *Aaron's Knock bound, which may also be a tinner's bound.*
Above right: *Stittleford Cross, Dunstone Manor boundary stone.*

and adjoining to Bittleford Parks Corner; thence to a junction of roads called Church Lane Head; from thence by the north side Cuckingford Mill; from thence along the boundary between Scobetor and Pulstone Down to William's Well; from thence in a straight line to Grey Goose Nest; from thence in a straight line to Stittlefords Cross; from thence by the Wall past Hensbury Gate to Seven Lords Land or Hallsbury, from thence to the north point of a Rock called Top Tor; from thence in a straight line to another Rock called Shovelstone and from thence in a straight line back to Rugglestone aforesaid.

The common boundary between the two manors was probably the River Webburn. It is interesting to note that by careful choice all of Wind Tor and Top Tor are inside the combined manors.

A number of the aforementioned points in the manor boundaries bear some form of marking. The Stittleford's Cross bound (Stentiford 1835), for example, is a rough pillar built into the wall engraved within a cross and the letters R.M. below (Rawlin Mallock of Cockington, who owned Dunstone Manor in 1748). By coincidence the letters M and R are engraved on Wind Tor. There is no marker at Two Crosses; it is said that two crosses were cut in the turf, but they would have had to be continually renewed. The name of the point itself could derive from it being a double crossroads, for tracks lead from here in the direction of Dockwell, Rowden, Kingshead, Southcombe (for Widecombe) and also Dunstone.

A NOTE ON DUNSTONE HOUSE

Following the publication of *Widecombe-in-the-Moor*, further details came to light with regards to Dunstone House by means of a letter from the now owner, Richard Large:

You make reference to the four medieval farms at Lower Dunstone and that one known as Wootens no longer exists. You say that your mother remembered its ruins lying behind Dunstone House when she saw it built in 1930. With all due respect I think you will find that it was not being built at that time although perhaps there were some works being carried out. You publish a photograph of Dunstone House, circa 1920, and the house is very much as it appears today (without the ivy which was apparently the culprit for a serious outbreak of dry rot in the early 1980s!). We have a very similar (but not identical) photograph obviously taken at the same time which we inherited from Mike and Jenny Pascoe from whom we purchased the house. The house actually must date to a considerable age although it was clearly renovated probably in the mid-Victorian period which included a new roof, windows and floors... The original stone walls are largely retained and are in places about three feet thick. The living-room fireplace which we uncovered is one of those formed by old granite slabs each side and it has an equally old wooden lintel. Even more interesting however is what appears to be a cruck roof timber in the main bedroom which is in line with the original gable wall facing the road (which was clearly much lower in the past than it is now). I strongly suspect that the cruck rafter is in its original location (which means it predates the granite chimney which it adjoins).

In the West Country Studies Library I have located Dunstone House on the 1885 edition of the Ordnance Survey plan, and the layout of the buildings is exactly as it was until we added an extension in 1995. The house must therefore have had its present-day plan at least from that time. All the evidence suggests that the house may well retain parts of the original medieval farmhouse on the site.

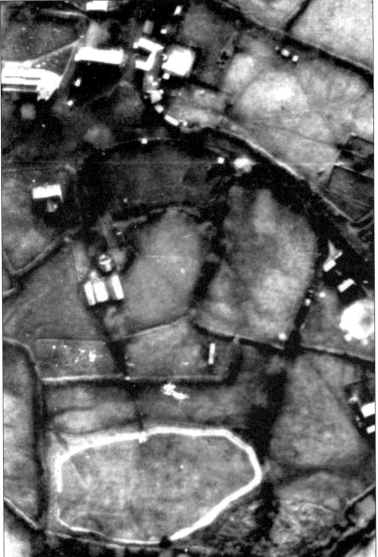

Included in Hermon French's collection was a photograph captioned 'In North Hall Great Moor, Widecombe', reproduced from R.A.F. aerial photo 2453, 10 Dec. 1946.' With it was what seemed to be a close-up of the moat and outlines of buildings inside, as well as the entrance – the site of the drawbridge (above).

The author contacted English Heritage and the National Monuments Record for a print of photo 2453. This covers a considerable area of land and includes Widecombe to Great Dunstone, to Dockwell, Hatchwell and just excludes Kingshead. An enlargement (left) was requested of part of the original to include the church, Widecombe village and North Hall Great Moor, to establish their relationship. This would appear to be the maximum enlargement possible before total breakup occurs.

The reader will see the difference between the two prints and will have to make up their own minds as to the interpretation of the close-up of North Hall. Copyright for photo 2453 lies with the R.A.F (Ministry of Defence) and the author is grateful for permission to use the image here.

Widecombe Town Manor

The Court Rolls of Widecombe for 1659 record the Widecombe Town Manor bounds as follows:

Also they p'sent that the bounds of the Commons belonging to the mannor of Widecombe doe lead lyneally from Hartsberry to Hawkeswell, and from thence to Hugh Clips Stone and so Northward. And that they doe leads Westward from Hartsberry to Norther Top Torr, And from thence to Shovel Stone, otherwise Thrylyestone and from thence to the highest part of Rugglestone and from thence to Hendystone and from thence to Cuddawell, and from thence to Two Crosses. And from thence to a blew stone neere Kingsett corner, And from thence to Harswell Neck and from thence to Stone Slade Tor, and from thence to the Ffyre beacon, and from thence eastward to a gray stone, att the head of Colemoor, and from thence to Vomaburrow, And from thence to Longa-knave, And from thence to Reedaworkes, And so to Brockadon hedge.

Over two centuries later, Henry Herbert Hannaford recorded the bounds in his 1896 diary (29 October) on his appointment as Reeve:

1. Henfoot Stone; 2. Rugglestone; 3. Shovel Stone; 4. Foxwell Seven Lords Land; 5. French Hanger/Hills Bay; 6. Cloven Rock; 7. Slades Well; 8. Ell Comer; 9. Broad Stone; 10. Long Reeve; 11. Old House; 12. Grey stone; 13. Hamilton Beacon; 14. Stone Slade Tor; 15. Herrings Knock; 16. Blue Stone; 17. Two Crosses; 18. Southcombe Well.

From Seven Lords Land it is not easy to follow the line to Clove Stone Rock but Robert Dymond points out the following route:

From Hartsberry, thence through Hedge Newtake along a reave and across the wall between Hedge Newtake and Bonehill Common to Clove Stone Rock.

The author remembers the reave well, but modern clearance has formed a series of man-made tors from its stones. However, the line of the reave can still be seen and cultivation often stops on its line.

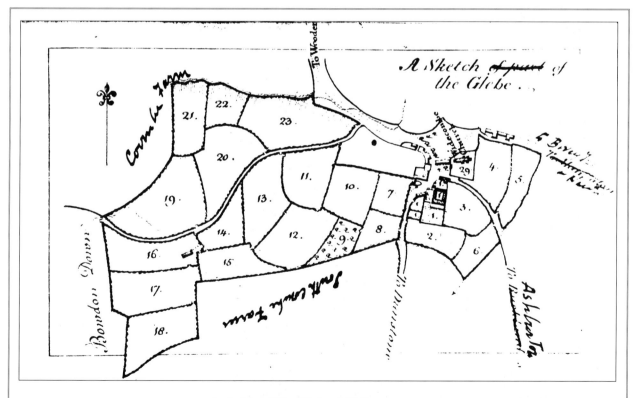

A sketch of the Glebe, 1815. (Keith Fox)

Seven Lords Land, a sepulchral circle. According to Robert Burnard the photograph shows Blackslade Down in the background but it is thought that it is probably Rippon Tor. The figure in the picture is Lawrie Headly. (Robert Burnard)

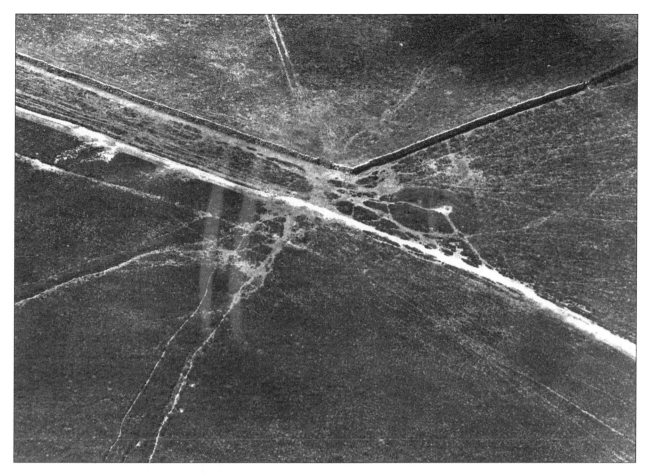

Two Barrow Bound. Note the ancient reave from the left joining the wall at the corner which continues as a wall/reave down towards the West Webburn in almost a straight line.

There is some doubt as to when Widecombe Town Manor came into being. There was no such establishment at Widecombe in 1086 as it was not mentioned in the Domesday Book (when the manors recorded in the parish were all farming communities). Sir Ralph Fitz Richard owned Widecombe Town Manor in and before 1283, in which year the family gave away the piece of land adjacent to Wodehay (sometimes Wooda and now known as Wooder) so that a church could be built upon it – one still stands there today.

At an auction in 1867, Mrs Drake (see 'The mysterious Lady Drake') purchased the manor and lands, which included an area associated with North Hall. During her time there she referred to the house simply as 'The Manor'; it is known today as Wooder Manor.

North Hall, first recorded in 1244, was owned by Sir Ralph and this may have been the original manor. Eric Hemery states 'Widecombe Town Manor (North Hall), but why Widecombe Town Manor remains a mystery.' North Hall is itself intriguing and little of its history is known. The site lies between the church lands and Wooder on an area known as North Hall Great Moor. The earth here has been considerably worked over and there is little to see on the ground.

In the 17th century, one Roger Hill wrote a poem about North Hall wherein he described the property as 'a messuage' which 'Tho' much decayed' contained:

Houses, courtlages, orchards, gardens, a stately grove of trees, all surrounded by a moat of clear water wherein good store of fish was bred.

Some 200 years later Robert Dymond recorded that there were people alive who remembered the ruined drawbridge by which the moat was crossed, facing towards the church. Among Hermon French's papers was an aerial photograph taken at 10 000 ft by the R.A.F. in 1946. Even with a 20-inch lens the image covers a considerable area and the moat is clearly discernible. With this was another print of North Hall, a substantial enlargement which shows what the author believes to be the outline of buildings within the moat and also the point at which the drawbridge stood. It is not an exact match for the R.A.F. photograph so unfortunately it is impossible to say for certain how it originated (*see page 80*).

Some of the boundary stones marked by the one-time owner of Natsworthy, Edward Augustus Seymour, during the 1850s. Clockwise from top: Pit boundary stone which stands beside the road at Natsworthy Gate; Grey Weather which stands next to what may have been the original boundary stone; Hameldown Cross boundary marker; Broad Burrow, which is also on the parish boundary; Hamilton Beacon; Long Knave, between Natsworthy and Widecombe Town manors; Slades Well boundary stone which is set next to a spring.

❧ Natsworthy Manor ❧

The lands of this manor lie on both sides of the valley of the East Webburn, known anciently as the Neparel. Those on the east flank of Hameldown were in 1566 owned by Lord Dynham and were part of Nottisworthy. A memorandum states:

THERE IS BELONGINGS TO THIS MANOR A GREATE WAST CONTEYNINGE BY ESTIMACION [–] ACRES AND IS BOUNDETH AS FOLLOWETH, THAT IS TO WETE:

From Hughston leadinge alonge by a certain rewe of the North parte unto Smalecomb and from thence along by the water of Smalecomb unto Smalecombe-hedde. And from thence unto Hollake necke of the North parte, and from thence unto the Thre Boroughes, and thence unto Fyerbicken of the West parte, and from thence towards the East along by Greyston to Colemoore-hedde, and from thence to Vome Borough, and from thence unto a dyche in the North parte, and from thence alonge by the Arable lands of the Tenements there of the East parte, towards the Northe.

During the 1850s, Natsworthy was owned by the Duke of Somerset, Edward Augustus Seymour, who at that time was an old man and nearing the end of his life. Perhaps because he knew this, a decision was made to mark out the manor boundary with neat cut stones engraved with the name of the manor on one side and the date, 'DS1854', on the other.

From Pit/DS1854 at Natsworthy Gate (there is a gravel pit near by) the line follows the East Webburn river up the flank of Hameldown to its source where stands the Blue Jug (the name of which remains as yet unexplained). Just above this is Grey Weather, or, as referred to by the Ordnance Survey, Grey Wethers. The old marker here was probably a boulder which stands next to the neatly inscribed stone. HC DS1854 was then cut on the much battered Hameldown Cross and the next points are the Thre Boroughes, Broad (also found on the parish boundary), Single and Two Barrows ('Burrow' in local dialect). Next comes Hamilton Beacon, which is also a marker for Widecombe Town Manor and which is referred to, in the 1722 Court Rolls, as 'Hamilton Beacon', in 1659 as a 'Ffyre beacon,' and in 1566 as 'Fyerbicken'.

The next marker on the boundary is referred to by Robert Dymond (1876) as 'Grey Wether Stone', but was called 'Gray Stone' in 1722, 'at the head of Colemoore' in 1659, and 'Greyston at Colemoore-hedde' in 1566. Despite this confusing array of names, the marker is hard to miss, standing as a large block of naturally shaped rock in the open waste.

The following marker is Old House, mentioned as such in 1722 in the Court Rolls, as 'Vomaburrow' in 1659, and as 'Vome Borough' in 1566. Continuing along the boundary one now descends the steep side of Hameldown to Long Knave. The latter is a corruption of local dialect; a steep-sided valley is a cleave, pronounced clave, and hence Knave. It is a sizeable pillar and one can, because of the angle of the slope, look down onto its top.

The names of the following handful of bounds have been subject to much change, although the line is fairly easy to follow. The boundary from Long Knave is, in Robert Dymond's version, as follows: 'A broad Rock in Bag Park, Pitt Parkes Bridge to L Corner' (most of which covers cultivated land).

Ell Corner, the first boundary stone out on the open moor, derives its name from the adjacent L-shaped field. From here, the bound crosses the saddle between Honeybags and Chinkwell tors, passing Slades Well on the way, the last of the DS1854 stones. There is a line of tin pits above, so it has been supposed that the 'Slade' of the well could have been a tinner who struck water, there being a spring here which makes a nice green patch. Anciently this would have been called a slade, so it remains uncertain as to whether the spot was first named after a person or the rising spring.

The boundary now crosses over to Clove Stone Rock (sometimes Saddle Rock), a natural boulder which has been split in two. In the ancient documents concerning Natsworthy many references are made to Brockendon which does not exist as such today. This name could be a corruption of 'broken down', 'broken down hedge' or reave, which became the estate of Hedge Barton and where there is a curious boundary line, with a West Lodge on the Widecombe Natsworthy road and an East Lodge under Hound Tor.

From Clove Stone Rock the Natsworthy boundary turns north then sharply west, before almost doubling back on itself eastward to meander through the fields and join the bridle path from Jays Grave to Natsworthy Gate and the Pit boundary stone. The author is not aware of any markers between Clove Stone Rock and Pit.

Clove Stone Rock – part of the Natsworthy Manor boundary.

Grey Wethers Stone, a natural granite boulder and part of Natsworthy Manor boundary.

❧ Spitchwick Manor ❧

The bounds of Spitchwick Manor were set out in 1752 as follows:

The Boundaries of This Manor of Spitchwick is Chiefly Bounded by the Rivers taking its Beginning at New Bridge at the South End thereof for the space of Three Miles or thereabout until we come to Wallabrooke foot from thence it is Bounded by the River Wallabrooke as for the space of Two Miles or Upward until you come to a Great Rock That layeth Near the 5d. River from whence it is bounded and is Lineable to a place Called Ring of Stones otherwise Ringaston at the North End thereof and from thence it is Bounded Lineable to a place called Southston Bye where there is a Little Lake of Water parteth the two Parishes of Widecombe and Manaton which 5d. lake of Water Emptieth itself into the River Wedbourn which River Boundeth the 5d. Mannor on the East side for the space of four or five miles until it comes to Buckland Bridge where the 5d. River Wedbourn Emptieth itsself into the River Dart which 5d. River Dart Boundeth the 5d. Manor at the South End thereof for about half a mile until we come to New Bridge where we begun.

The 'Great Rock' bound is not is existence but opposite where the old wooden caravan stood is a sett stone, now with a bronze plaque which aligns on an ancient reave that follows the boundary to the junction of two church paths near Ephraims Pinch. The reave forms the boundary line of Widecombe and Manaton Parishes, Spitchwick Manor, and also a Cator Estate. In its length are three bound stones engraved CB Cator Bound.

This line does not go to a 'Ring of Stones' but north of the boundary and kept outside Soussons Plantation is a fine cairn circle and cist. If one follows a line through this stone circle over the ridge one finds oneself descending to the West Webburn along the little stream known as Widecombe Lake. It is also interesting to note that beside the road at Ephraims Pinch is a fourth CB stone which is outside the line of the present boundary.

Part of a page from the Spitchwick Manor Book for 1786.

97

Beating the bounds of Spitchwick Manor, 17 May 1924, at Dartmeet. Charlie French is having his head wetted in the river by Phillip Brain (left) and Jack Cleave (right). Standing on the rocks are George Hannaford? (left) and Sam Cannon (right). (Iris Woods)

Above left: *Cator boundary stone set in its rightful position on the line of Spitchwick Manor boundary and also Widecombe and Manaton parish boundaries.*
Above right: *This prominent boundary stone near Ephraim's Pinch has, for some reason, been left out of the current agreed boundary for both Spitchwick Manor and Widecombe Parish.*

The cairn circle on the edge of Soussons Plantation was used as a bound in 1752 and was referred to as 'Ring of Stones otherwise Ringaston'.

Newbridge, c.1930. (Sylvia Needham)

Cockingford, 1960. (Marnie Lentern)

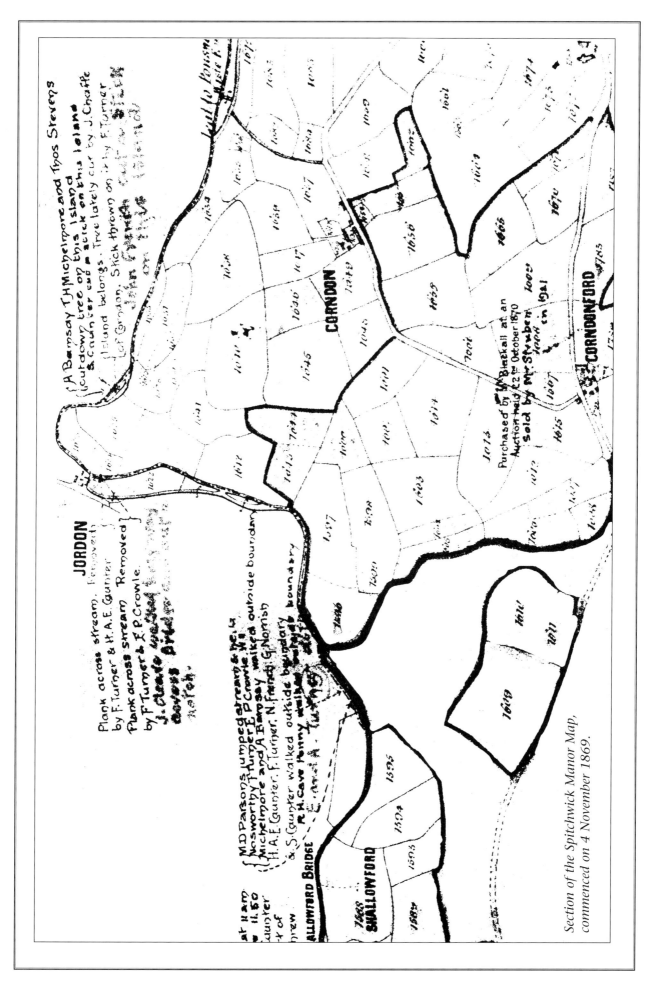

*Section of the Spitchwick Manor Map,
commenced on 4 November 1869.*

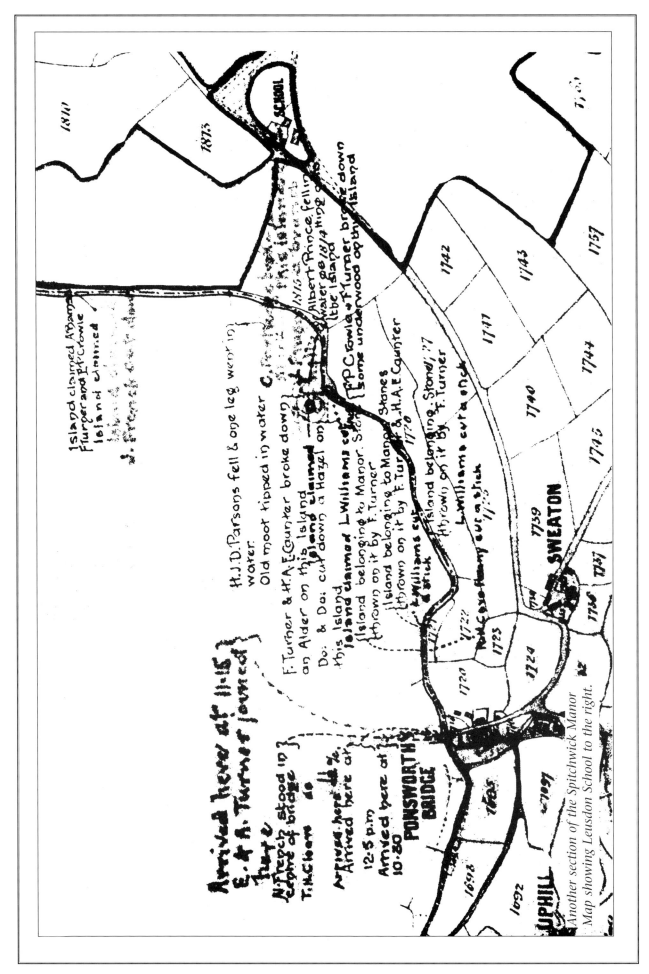

Another section of the Spitchwick Manor Map showing Leusdon School to the right.

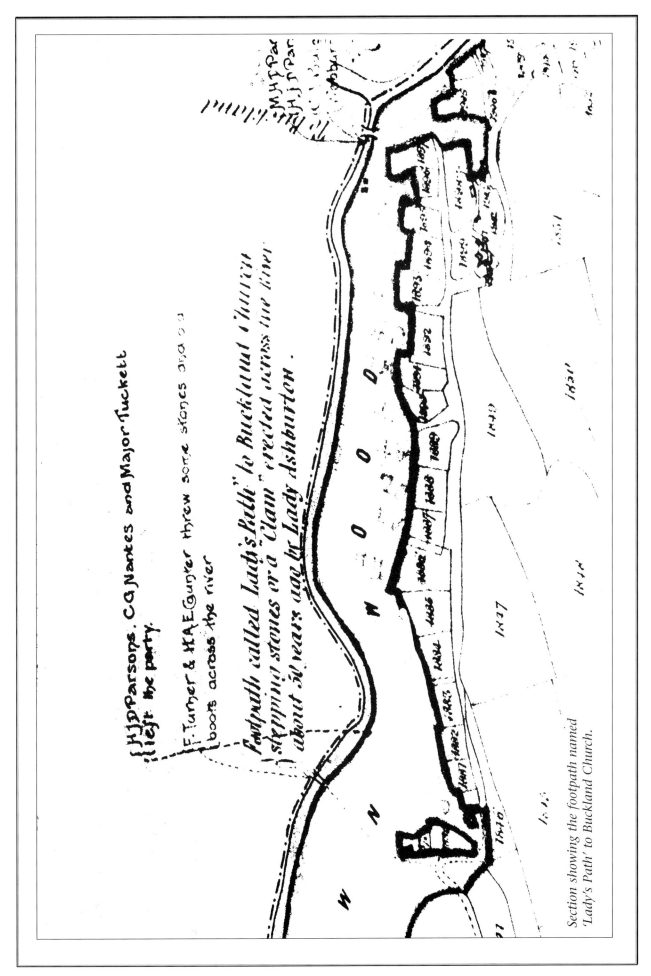

Section showing the footpath named 'Lady's Path' to Buckland Church.

Buckland Lower Lodge.

Mary Caunter of Ollsbrim.

FRANK DYMOND, STEWARD OF SPITCHWICK MANOR: THE GREAT BLIZZARD OF 1891

Just after noon on Monday 9 March 1891 a violent snow storm descended on the South West and continued for 30 hours. As William Crossing later stated, it decimated the rabbit population. The Great Western Railway line was closed down until 11 March when, with the aid of snow ploughs and an army of men, it was re-opened to Newton Abbot – although the service to Totnes and the branch line (now run as a tourist attraction) to Ashburton was to remain closed until the Friday.

Frank Dymond was steward to Dr Blackall, lord of Spitchwick Manor, and a younger brother to Robert Dymond. He felt it his duty to attend the annual rent audit and dinner dance set for Thursday 12 March, the tenantry having been summoned to appear. Accompanied by his 'Clerk B', wearing heavy overcoats and carrying the necessary estate books, Frank set off to the manor. The pair went by train to Newton Abbot, arriving on time, at about 3 p.m. and made their way to the Globe Hotel, where they hired a two-wheeled dog-cart and driver and, because of the conditions, took a second horse harnessed in tandem.

Conditions were not too bad to begin with and they passed the Halfway House on the Newton-Ashburton road without any problems, but soon the road became impassable with a 12-foot-deep drift of snow stretching away into the distance. Seeing that the fields above the road appeared reasonably clear, the men left their dog-cart and, carrying the books, set out over the fields making their way, not without a struggle, to Ashburton, through snow that at times was 19 inches deep. At the Golden Lion Hotel they enquired about the road conditions to New Bridge and were told that the postman had only been able to go as far as Holne Bridge. Knowing that there was a carriageway from Holne Bridge through Buckland Woods and past Lovers Leap to the Lower Lodge, and knowing their friend Mr Bastard of Buckland Court would allow them to go that way if it was passable, the men decided to try.

Having procured horses and a man, they started out down the pavements which had been cleared, the snow being piled high in the streets with cross cuts at regular intervals. They made their way out onto the open road to Holne Bridge at about 6.30 p.m. The snow was much deeper than that which they had met with before and at one point the road was blocked by 10-foot drifts which they rounded by entering the adjacent fields and travelling across country until they could regain the road. Eventually they reached Holne Bridge. Mr Bastard's private road to the Lodge is about 1½ miles long and stretches first across two open fields then through the woods, climbing 100 feet to pass just behind the precipitous rocks of Lovers Leap from whence it descends to the Lodge near the confluence of the Webbern and Dart at Buckland Bridge.

By the time that sunset had passed and darkness was well on the way, the two men had managed fairly well to pass Lovers Leap having at times dismounted to remove snow-laden and broken branches in their path. Then they found a fallen tree blocking the way. On one side the bank fell 50 feet to the river and on the other it rose nearly vertically away into the darkness.

Ascertaining that they could go under the trunk they sent the man back with the horses, while wading slowly forward through two feet of snow, hampered by their luggage and heavy overcoats. Eventually a dense fence of foliage weighed down with snow blocked their way. Dymond had travelled this way many times and knew no such fence existed; he also realised that they must be near the Lodge but attempts to go around were thwarted by the dense undergrowth. Later the barrier was found to be the ornamental laurels that stood beside the track but which, weighed down with snow, formed an impenetrable wall.

By this time it was past 9 p.m. and very dark. When a dog was heard to bark, their shouts of 'Hello there' set off a whole pack of hounds, which in turn awoke the occupants of the Lodge, who had retired early. Soon lights appeared and a few minutes later Dymond and his man were in the kitchen. The fire was brought to life and hot food and drinks provided.

In the morning Dymond, having found out from a neighbour it would take three hours to cut a way through the snow up to the Manor House, abandoned his attempt to attend the Manor Court as no one else, he was assured, would attempt to be there either. He and his clerk struggled back to Ashburton and on to Exeter. Dymond ends his narrative, on 15 March 1891, with the words:

Thus ended in failure the attempts to keep my appointment for the Spitchwick rent audit on Thursday 12th March 1891. I had at any rate gained a new experience and amongst other things had learned from it that at the age of 65½ years I no longer possessed the muscular vigour and power of endeavour which were mine in earlier days.

Whether he returned to collect the rents is not known but he was certainly recorded in the Spitchwick Manor Book for the Jury and Homage the following year. Knowing these hardy individualists it was not surprising to hear Sylvia Needham relate that William Norrish of Combestone Farm invariably paid his rent in gold and at the annual rent dinner would lick his plate clean!

Huccaby Bridge from Dartmoor Illustrated, *T.A. Falcon, 1900.*

Postbridge Clapper from Dartmoor Illustrated, *T.A. Falcon, 1900.*

Chapter 8: Lanes and Byways

As mentioned in *Widecombe-in-the-Moor*, the magistrates fined the parish the cost of road repairs and gave the money to the waywardens who saw to it that the work was done. Below are two further examples from the court and waywardens' records:

Quarter Sessions – Withecombe-in-the-Moor

Easter 1804 – the road in length ³/₄ of a mile from a certain plot of ground in the said parish of Withecombe-in-the-Moor called Greensplot home to a certain other plot of ground called Sandys Plot in the same parish in the road leading from the town of Ashburton in the county aforesaid towards and unto Chagford.

Witness Rich. Parry
Midsummer 1805 - Discharged by Mr Barrington's C.cil.

The following appears in the Widecombe accounts:

1804: Paid ye cost of Inditement	16/6
ditto	£1.15.6
Journey to Exeter	7/6
1805: Expenses of an Inditement of the road	
Council fee	£2.2.0
Attorney's fee	10/6
Clark of the Peace two sessions	16/-
Cryer of Court	6d

Clark of Peace	£3.5.4
And three journeys	£1.2.6
Two days there and Chudleigh	£1.10
	16/6
	£1.15.6

The piece of road that required repairing was, the author believes, Widecombe Hill, from where the road left the fields above the Southway turning to Haresfoot Cross on what was then the old carter's track from Ashburton to Chagford.

An earlier inditement also makes fascinating reading:

Quarter Sessions – Withecombe-in-the-Moor

Michaelmas 1798 – the road containing in length about 3 miles and half and in breadth 16 ft from a place called Cherrybrook to the New House in Dartmoor. [Note the extra breadth, 16 ft, this being the 1772 Turnpike, and New House, the previous structure to the Warren House Inn.].

Witness Bryan Roberts Faster 1799 Respited Midsummer 1799 Traversed, Easter 1800 Acquitted

The accounts read:

1799: To Wm. French going to Exeter and abiding 3 days	18/
Fees of Court	8/4
A man for Witness	1/4

The Warren House Inn. (Kath Brewer)

A small paper-covered notebook from Hermon French's collection sets out the roads maintained in the parish giving their lengths and the various points between which they were measured. It also gives those tracks which it is thought were previously looked after by the way-wardens but which, with an increase in wheeled traffic, became disused. The name J. Hannaford, Widecombe, appears inside the front cover, but there is neither a date nor an explanation of the book's purpose. The short section on roads begins:

Cost of maintaining and keeping Roads in Repair, etc. since the foundation of the Highway Boards. The Average of the three years before the formation of the said Boards was £85.9.4.

To December 31	1864	£59.1. 9
"	1865	£91.1. 5
"	1866	£109.7. 4
"	1867	£182.–.1½
"	1868	£260.–. 5
"	1869	£189.5.11
"	1870	£166.9. 1
"	1871	£175.8. 1
"	1872	£231.17.1

It is then explained in the notebook that after the waywardens gave up the responsibility of the Forest Quarter the parish was still divided into four sections called Coombe, Dewdon, North Spitchwick and South Spitchwick. Note that Dewdon had not then been replaced by the present Jordan, although both Jordan and Jordan Gate are recorded. The notebook then contains a precise record of the separate road lengths within each section (as well as the grand totals, *above*):

Measurement of roads Widecombe-in-the-Moor

No.1 Coombe Division	M	F	Yds
The Chagford exactly	1	-	-
From the Chagford Road to Widecombe Town	1	1	39
From Northway Bridge to Bunhill Down Gate		7	4
From Sandy Plot to Thornhill Lane End	1	4	10
Widecombe Town to Natsworthy Head	2	4	36
(This road is marked by the 1 mile post)			
From Blackslade Ford to Blackslade		5	-
From Chittleford Down Gate to Widecombe Town	1	2	38
From Bowden Gate to Kingshead Corner		6	2
(the commencement of the church path to Pizwell			
and might have had a gate post incised with a cross –			
now used as a gate post to Kingshead Farm)			
From Two Crosses to Southcombe Lane End		4	26
Widecombe Town to Church Lane Head	1	-	28
From Chittleford to Dunstone Lane End		3	2
Church Lane Head to Cockingford		2	6
Total Coombe	12	2	31

No. 2 Dewdon Division			
From Church Lane Head to Ponsworthy	1	0	39
From the bottom of Easter Lane to Rowden Cross	1	0	17
From Rowden Cross to Rex Bridge	1	1	18
Waybrige to Three gates		1	18
From Challacombe Cross to Blue Gate		5	15
From Rowden Cross to Blackaton Coombe Bridge	1	7	5
From Three Gates by Broadaford to the bottom of			

Frenches Lane		6	13
From Easter Lane Gate to Shallaford Bridge	1	1	10
From Crossgate thro Dockwell to Two Crosses		6	12
From Crossgate by Jordan gate		5	29
From Blackaton Coombe bridge to Pizwell Ford	1	1	37
Total Dewdon	10	6	13

No. 3 North Division of the Spitchwick Quarter

From Locks Gate to Cator South Gate	1	7	29
From Cator Southgate to Pizwell Ford	1	0	37
From Rexbridge to Coakers Hill		7	37
Waybridge to Cator Hill Gate		3	19
Pepper Lane head to Shollaford Bridge		2	23
Shollaford South Way		1	30
From Babeny Brook to Sherwell		3	37
From Sherwell to Ollsbrim Cross	1	1	14
From Ollsbrim Brake Corner to Forderbridge	1	0	33
(on this route stands a mile stone engraved W3 Widecombe 3 Miles)			
From Uppacott Butts to Locksgate		5	6
Locksgate			7
Total North Division of Spitchwick Quarter	8	3	32

No. 4 South Division of Spitchwick Quarter

From Rowbrook to Belltor Corner		6	34
From the County Stone Ponsworthy to Park Lane Head	1	0	21
From Town Lane End to New Close Corner			32
From the Cross near Mrs Larpent's to Town Village		4	-
Hillgate to Buckland Road		6	24
From Buckland boundary to Baring Hill		5	3
From Newbridge to Park Lane Head	1	2	12
From Park Lane Head to Dartmeet Bridge	2	2	17
Uppacott to Torr		2	18
From Middle Hannaford to Newbridge		3	30
Total South Division of Spitchwick Quarter	8	2	31

Roads not maintained by the Parish

Kingshead Corner to Claypark Corner		6	-
Rowden Cross to Two Crosses		3	11
Bittleford Down Lane		1	31
From Frenches Gate to Two Crosses		5	6
Path over Cator Commons leading to Runnagbridge	1	0	8
Heath Cross to Grendon		3	26
Locksgate to Corndon		3	-
Path over Leusdon leading to Leusdon Chapel		1	27
Ash Lane			7
Lake Lane			19
Uppacott North Road			8
From Newbridge Hill to Middle Hannaford		3	30
Total	4	5	13

Temperance Hotel, Postbridge, on the Tavistock Turnpike Trust. (Chapman & Son)

The road-menders pause for refreshment. On the left is Bill Bray and on the right is George Ford.
(Beatrice Chase, 1931)

The Warren House Inn during the 1930s. Standing at 1400 feet, it is recorded on this postcard as 'the second highest inn in England'. (Kath Brewer)

A postcard by E.S. London (no. 485) of the Warren House Inn, postmarked 1907. (Kath Brewer)

Sherberton Bridge, 1892. Both the road to Sherberton and this bridge were maintained by the waywarden for the Forest Quarter which was later taken over by the Tavistock Trust. (Robert Burnard)

The ancient tenement of Sherburton, 1892. Mrs Coaker and her children are standing in the doorway. (Robert Burnard)

The steep gradients and the effects of rainwater were the main causes of damage to the roads.

1783: For repairing road Thomas Bards newtack in Hartter Lane. For cleansing of the Drens and bytables and tacking care of the Watter in ditto.

Tacking care of the watter that might not hert the road between Park Corner and Widdecum Town.

Gutters, Bytables and drens and tacking care of watter in road between Newbrig and Dunabrig pound.

It is also interesting when reading the accounts to note the changes in working methods and procedures:

1782: For blowing of a rock 1/6
1783: At Torr for cleaving and firing rocks 4/-
1799: Pd to Edward Stranger his salary for repairing of Jolly by contract and 5 years more to come of his term. He is to receive 6/- per year.
1799: To Wm. French for repairing road between Dartmit and Dunabridge Farm and keeping same in good repair, yearly salary to be £2.12.6 the term to end at Michaelmas 1804.
1803: Pd for blowing 46 ft of rock in Bunhill Lane at 6d per foot.
1837: William Leaman for breaking 37 cartloads of stone and putting them abroad on the Chagford road at 6d per load.

In the Widecombe accounts from 1769 we learn that there were those who did extra statutory labour 'in lieu of horse and cart' – the cart not necessarily being a wheeled vehicle but possibly a sledge (or 'slide' as it was known). In the way-warden's account for 1776 we find this reference:

Paid Ambrose Nosworthy for shewing of a Stone Dry twice 1/-
Ditto for staving a Dry 4d
Paid Richard Bulley for shewing a Slide on to and staving the same 10d

'For shewing' refers to the fitting of metal runners to a sledge for pulling stones; the staves are the wooden cross members. Other references to vehicles are few and far between: '1784: For blowing of a rock that was in the way of the

John 'Granfer' Dawe at upper Lydgate. Among other things, he acted as a guide to visitors. (Eileen Exell and Dorothy Williams)

carriages at Withecombe town.' (This is believed to refer to the rocks at the west end of the Church House, part of the foundation of the Sexton's cottage which jut out into the road between the Church House and the Old Inn, probably at the opposite end to the upping stock.). In 1795 there is record of a bill 'For repairing the Ford for the cart to come through at Babeny,' and in the Burial Registers for 1846 one Richard Smerdon (13) is recorded as having been killed on 18 May 'by a cart running over him'. His brother, John (15), died on the same day but no explanation is given for this.

Earlier reference to wheeled transport survives in the form of the will of 'Arthur Aptor of Widecombe in the County of Devon, Yeoman'. Dated 1659, it contains a bequest made to Arthur's grandson (also called Arthur) of '£5 and the wheels of my waine.' Arthur Aptor also owned lands off the moor at Ashburton and his waine may have been used on those lands. There is also one other interesting recording which was made by the Widecombe waywardens for 9 March 1773: 'Mr Dunning for his oxen and cart 4 days 10/-'. This is the only reference to oxen in Widecombe but Mr Dunning was of high stature, being an eminent lawyer who became the first Lord Ashburton.

In 1772 an Act was passed which referred to:

Repairing and improving the roads from the town and borough of Tavistock through Cherrybrook to Moretonhampstead and also from Two Bridges to Dunnabridge Pound on the road from Tavistock to Ashburton and other places.

The Act through which the Turnpike Trust was set up was put through Parliament by Mr Turner, the Duke of Bedford's steward, in spite of objections from Okehampton and towns on the Cornish border. There were, in fact, two trusts, Tavistock and Moretonhampstead which covered the roads described above. Exactly where their jurisdiction met has not been discovered, but it could well be that there was a buffer zone between the two, for although outside the parish of Widecombe, parts of these roads were the responsibility of the waywarden of the Forest Quarter. The Tavistock Trust gets several mentions in the accounts:

1787: Expended for myself (John Cleave) and horse in going to Tavystock to carry over the list of inhabitants of this parish that pay to the high ways and for writing out the list 2/6

1788: Paid to the Troste of the tornpick at Tavistock £4

1789: To Tavistock Truss for repairing of road between Hexworthy and Sherborn £2.2

This last is an intriguing entry as the Act refers specifically to the Turnpike going to Dunnabridge Pound and this road is on the far side of the Dart. The most likely explanation is that because the Forest Dwellers paid towards the upkeep of the Trust that the body agreed to oversee their roads.

1791: To Tavystock Trust £2.2

1796: Towards a journey to Tavistock as part and part towards a summons 1/10d

1797: Trust of turnpike of Tavistock £2.2. Going to pay same 3/6

1800: Received of last surveyor money which he charged on his account to pay Tavistock Trust and not demanded £2.2

It is worth mentioning here another route called the Mariners Way which was the path followed by sailors walking from the port of Bideford on the North Devon coast to Dartmouth on the English Channel. Its route descended the Widecombe Valley and references are made in the accounts to subsistence payments for the sailors making their way south:

1719: Gave to poor seaman 1/-
Given to two poor sailors that had a certificate to ask relief 1/-

1725: 9 seaman which had a petition to beg 1/8

It is surprising how many people drifted on the tracks through Widecombe, many of them with a sad story to tell:

1716: Given to a poor woman whose husband and home were burnt
Given to a poor dumb man

1725: To 2 travellers from the county of Essex whose county was drowned and had a petition to beg 2/-"

1726: Given to 2 travellers which was burnt out of house and home and having a petition under 2 or 3 justices hands to travel and ask alms 7/6

A somewhat cryptic memorandum appears at the end of the 1726 accounts:

This is to certify that at a p'ish meeting it is agreed that there is nothing to be allowed by ye p'shoners to ye Churchwardens for bringing home any bell rope or ropes, nor to give anything to any Travellers which ask alms.

Whatever it was that upset the parishioners it was soon forgotten and payments continued to be made to travellers passing through the parish.

Above: *A visitor in her motor car outside the Warren House Inn.* (Eileen Exell and Dorothy Williams)

Left: *A sign on the gate at Pizwell Bridge during the Second World War. It reads: 'Please shut gate. Meat rations will stray.* (Liz Fursdon)

Chapter 9: Tourism

Widecombe farmer's wives have long played an active part in the family economy. In times gone by, their jobs would seem endless, from feeding the chickens and collecting the eggs, to scalding the milk and making cream, butter and any other commodities that could be sold at market or over the garden gate. Another source of income was the offering of a night's lodging with a substantial meal in the morning. B&B, as we know it today, is a thriving industry. Next came the conversion of outbuildings for self-catering holiday. Angela Bell of Wooder, for example, converted the stables there into a series of self-contained flats named after the local tors, Chinkwell and Honeybags.

Over the last few years the camping barn has sprung up. These barns offer basic accommodation at a low price. Runnage, where the Coakers have farmed for several generations, was one of the first to offer this form of accommodation and now has two barns on offer for individuals and small groups.

The author is very grateful to Kate Van Der Kiste for bringing to his attention the diaries of a group of visitors who stayed at Ponsworthy House in 1888 and 1889, as well as to Mary Rivers-Moore, the present custodian of 'A Record of our Adventures' which are quoted here. The main protagonists were the Organist (Organiser and Fisherwoman) – in real life Marion Moore, daughter of Dowager Lady Freeling, and wife of William Foster Moore, three times Mayor of Plymouth. She took the name Rivers-Moore by deed poll in 1905 and is the author of the record. The 'Tramp' was Jane Risk and the 'Artist' Miss Greta Bond (although most of the sketches in 'A Record of Our Adventures' were painted by the Organist).

The group began their adventures on Tuesday 12 June 1888, their party consisting of 'three horses, three babies, three maidservants, three matrons, two girls and two grooms':

Our great idea being to travel with light luggage, we have only nineteen parcels in the van, and nine small packages in our carriage... three of the parcels are represented by Baths. The comfort of the elders too being a great consideration, we have provided several easy chairs: two of the remaining packages

The Tramp, 1888.
(Rivers-Moore diaries)

contain wine, tinned meats, soups, and other luxuries not to be procured in the wilds of Dartmoor.

The accounts of their day-to-day outings make it clear that the tracks and open wastes they travelled upon are today tarmac roads, and that their costumes were those of respectable, upper-class Victorian ladies, used to riding side saddle or driving carriages. The first day was spent easily:

The Artist was left by the Tramp and Organist on her collapsible seat, sketching the village of Ponsworthy which consists of about six cottages, a bridge dated 1666, a forge, one shop wherein you can buy an antiquated orange, Sunlight soap, cocoa, one pot of marmalade, and sweets generally detached from the sides of the bottles by a knife which has been used to cut up bacon.
The Tramp and the Organist went on their way which led them by the side of the West Webburn river, until they came to a most original, and crazy bridge called by the natives a 'Clam' (? because you have to clamber over). This bridge consists of the trunk of a slight tree, to which was attached a handrail which shook when touched, but which this time allowed the explorers to get safely across... The evening was enlivened by sweet strains from the piano accompanied by the Organist and Musician (otherwise Tramp). The said piano (a most valuable Steinway which please keep locked) had arrived from Ashburton in the morning.

The party was subjected to a great deal of rain but managed to visit Hay Tor, Hound Tor, Bonehill Rock, Holne, Huccaby, Dartmeet, Grimspound and Postbridge. The trip to the latter was typical; having reached 'Belliver Farm' the road, which hitherto had been as good as could have been wished, suddenly evaporated and the ladies:

... had to drive on following the children's path to school [before arriving] at the Inn to find it inundated with six gig-fuls of tourists.

The drive to Holne Cott was also eventful:

Our usual dashing speed was checked by a stage

Leightor

Charbetor (Bonehill Rocks, named Charbetor by the group), Bell, Chinkwell and Honeybags.

Houndtor

Haytor Rocks

Rippon Tor Logan Stone

Sharp Tor

Huccaby Bridge

Rushford Mill stepping stones on the River Teign at Chagford.

The Dart Gorge seen from Bench Tor.

The barn at Lizwell Farm.

Ponsworthy Mill complete with thatch.

Postbridge Clapper with the ruins of the barracks in the background.

❧ Ponsworthy ❧

Left: *Ponsworthy from* Dartmoor Illustrated, *T.A. Falcon, 1900.*

Below: *Ponsworthy village from the air.*

Bottom left: *A postcard by Chapman & Son of 1916 showing a horse and trap at the entrance to Ponsworthy House.* (Iris Woods)

Bottom right: *Back yard and stables at Ponsworthy House, 1888.* (Rivers-Moore diaries)

coach, and a supplementary break which dawdled on before us thro' the narrow lanes... At Hexworthy bridge our Tramp here wanted to know if there were any more gates to open, as she was quite faint and giddy with jumping in and out of the carriage for which she did not even get a half penny. At the end of the drive, the poor Tramp calculated that she had opened at least 10 gates.

They obviously enjoyed themselves for they were back again in 1889 for another month's holiday, at the end of which whey went over to Chagford for a trip to Cranmere Pool:

Saturday, 10th August 1889, was a real red letter day, for the Trio (The Tramp, The Organist and The Item [Emmy Lowth, a member of the Rivers family] really did get to Cranmere Pool! They started in a small but strong one-horse waggonette driven by Perrott junior (below). They passed thro' Fernworthy, and then all track over the moor was lost. They floundered about over rocks and boulders in a helpless sort of fashion, and the driver must have his way by instinct as the rain was so thick, all the landmarks were blotted out. At length, after a very jolty drive, they saw an isolated cottage inhabited by a shepherd and his wife: the latter was very kind and hospitable.

Their way grew wetter and wetter till all hope of keeping dry was given up. No mackintosh could keep out such rain, and their skirts being kilted up high to avoid the bog, the Trio's boots were soon full of water. The wind, too, blew in its strength, driving rain into every fold and crevice, but still they manfully struggled over the pathless waste.

They went Indian file. Guide first: the Tramp next, her long legs carrying her close to the guide, after an interval came the Organist and Item.

After a toilsome ascent, a ruined cottage was reached, called 'Mutine' from some Swiss peasants who once lived there cutting peat for making charcoal. After this, the bona fide bog was reached: splish, splosh went they through what looked like nice green grass at a short distance. Presently, the grass grew more scattered, and the wet stood between the tussocks of grass. The ground became more and more broken, and black boggy fissures yawned beneath the travellers' feet; sometimes these could be jumped over; sometimes they had to be waded thro'. No water ran there, but black oozy mud lay at the bottom which had to be stepped upon lightly, cautiously, but quickly as the foot sank rapidly beneath the surface.

No four-footed animal can stand upon this thin layer of grass and rushes, which is all that lies between the traveller and 20 feet of black quivering bog! This kind of ground, with variations, was all the Trio met with till they reached their destination.

Mr Standford Perrott with his son John S. Perrott and two children. (Beatrice Chase, 1931)

'There rises the Dart.'

'Here is the source of the Taw.'

On and on, step by step they toiled; reached the brow of the hill; struggled on a short way; and then shouts: 'I see it! I see it! I see it!' from the Trio, and the goal was reached, the dream of Tramp's life was fulfilled. They stood in Cranmere Pool. There was a small cairn of stones erected by Perrott, and concealed in the cairn was a tin case, and in the case a little book in which adventurous few who reach Cranmere Pool inscribe their names. The Trio of course added theirs to the roll call of heroes and heroines of Cranmere.

They could not stay long as they were thoroughly wet thro', and feared standing about and getting chilled. Right glad were they to see the top of the chimney of the cottage rising out of the valley below them and, collecting all their jaded powers, they scrambled down to its hospitable shelter. Mrs Liddle (or Little), the shepherd's wife, was most kind and helped them to try and dry their sodden clothes.

Close to the cottage runs a branch of the Teign crossed only by a foot bridge, and it had to be forded by vehicles.

'I'm glad we were safe over that river', said Perrott, 'I was afraid it would be so swollen we should not be able to cross it. In another half-hour that stream will be a roaring torrent.'

They jolted, bumped, and floundered thro' the marshy and bouldery land between the river and Fernworthy, being tossed about like dried peas on parchment; and then, having gained the hard road, they fell to singing all the glees and trios they knew

to keep themselves from thinking how wet and cold they were.

They arrived at the Moor Park Hotel like drowned rats, but saying in tones of triumph 'We did it! We did it!' they rushed in demanding hot water, hot drinks, and hot baths: dashed upstairs to their rooms, and were seen no more till they appeared at the dinner table clothed in their right minds, and overflowing with triumph.

Some considerable time ago the group's diary became lost to the family when a teacher from Newcastle saw it and bought it for his parents who had just moved to South Devon. The couple decided that it would be nice to try to trace the Rivers family, which they did, and it is now the proudest possession of Mary Rivers-Moore.

1921, picnicking at Cranmere Pool. Jack Symons is on the left with his back to the camera, in the centre is John 'Granfer' Dawe, and on the right is Dorothy James.

A photograph by Chapman & Son of Ponsworthy House (on the hill to the left of the road) where the Organist, the Tramp and the Artist stayed. (Suzanne Hutchins)

❧ Dartmeet ❧

Dartmeet is as popular a place with today's tourists as it was with the Victorians. The Dymonds recorded many visits to the spot as did the Ponsworthy sojourners. On 20 June 1889 they recorded:

As soon as possible after lunch, the party started for Dartmeet Bridge taking the two elder children with them, the Organist and the Tramp were riding and, on nearing Dartmeet Bridge, they went on to reconnoitre and find the cottage where tea could be made.

'Let's go on and enquire at the cottage,' said the Organist, pointing to a pretty little house on the right; so accordingly, they cantered off to make enquiries.

At the garden gate a gentleman greets them somewhat to their embarrassment, as he evidently is a gentleman both in manner and aspect, while they expected their host to be – well – not quite so refined. 'Pardon me,' says our Organist, with her usual politeness, 'but is this house a Tea House?'

'No,' is the reply, 'but it's a grog shop' – most perplexing man.

'Then does a man named Caunter live here?'

'No' is again the answer, 'This is the Badger's Hole, and I am the Badger!'

'We apologise profusely for our mistake.'

'Don't mention it,' says the Badger. 'Come in and have tea with me.'

We demurred at this, however, and asked where the real tea house was to be found. Having identified the cottage and while tea was made, we looked about.

Dartmeet looked lovely, and the Artist and Organist set to work at once to sketch while the Tramp and her mother wander about admiring the lovely views. The Organist's mother sat on a chair which had been brought out from the little cottage, and the two small boys proceeded to fill up the Dart by energetically throwing in stones – an amusement which did not flag the whole afternoon.

We had tea down by the river, after which we were compelled to hasten homewards as the mist is descending around us. Mrs Caunter at the cottage tells us that the Badger's name is Rose and that he is hospitality itself giving tea to any passing strangers who care to partake of his kindness.

Nowadays one can get cream teas or lunches at Badger Holt or climb the hill to Brimpts. Most bring their own food and sit on the river's bank

Ruth James (driver), employee of Robert Wallace who owned Pixies Holt. Also in the car is Ruth's daughter, Dorothy. (Eileen Exell and Dorothy Williams)

Above: *Dorothy James (third from the left, back) as a day student at Greycoat Hospital School.*

Above right: *Dorothy on Miss Collins-Platt's donkey with her mother and dogs Trout and Truff at Brimptsmead.*

Above: *Dorothy as a little girl with Miss Caunter (Mrs Jane Cross), known as the 'Belle of the Moor', 1914.*

Right: *Dorothy and Eileen Exell's grandmother, Dorothy Dawe, with her sister Margaret, at Princetown School, 1893/4. The two girls are at the far right, back row. Eileen's grandchildren attend the same school today.*

A photograph by Jerome Dessain & Co. of Pixies Holt, Dartmeet, and (right) the Dart in spate. (Eileen Exell and Dorothy Williams)

while younger members clamber over the stones and on to the clapper bridge or simply throw stones at the river. The energetic can visit the Coffin Stone or clamber higher on Vaghill and hunt for vermin traps among the ancient reaves.

The author has spent some time looking to see if the pattern at Postbridge; ford, stepping stones, medieval foot bridge and turnpike/county bridge is repeated here. The latter two are here, and somewhere there was a ford but no one has recorded stepping stones in the vicinity.

Two tinners, Christopher Prous and Richard Hamlyn, leased an acre of land hereabouts in 1514, the bounds of which were the Derta (Dart), a spring called Hangerwille, and the path from Greneaway to Smethaford. Within the acre there was:

Also a myll there called a blowyng myll and knacking myll with the weir and stream of water flowing to the said myll which Christopher and Richard lately built there.

In 1514 then, the site was used both for crushing 'tin stuff' as it came out of the ground and for refining the ore in a furnace.

If you cross the bridge east to west, about 200 yards up the hill on the left is Pixies Holt, a shooting lodge owned by Robert Wallace before the First World War. At the top of the hill past the turning to Huccaby on the right is Huccaby Cottage, formerly known as Mazedman (or Meresman) Cottage.

The road to the left which crosses the beautiful old pack-horse bridge and climbs steeply up past the Forest Inn was known as Jolly. Opposite Jolly Lane Cot is The Bearas where two charming ladies, Mrs Eileen Exell and Mrs Dorothy Williams, reside. Mrs Eileen Exell (née Willcocks) was born in 1923 and her parents were Frank and Dorothy Willcocks (née Dawe). Dorothy Williams (née James) was born in 1909 and her parents were George and Ruth James (née Dawe). They therefore share the same grandparents, John 'Granfer' Dawe and Mary Dawe (née Durrant).

George James was employed by Robert Wallace of Pixies Holt as a chauffeur and gardener. At the outbreak of the First World War he went to serve his country and did not return. His wife Ruth took over as chauffeur and was driving a car well before the Hannafords of Southcombe bought theirs.

Robert Wallace took his responsibilities to his employee very seriously and had Dorothy educated, at his own expense, at the Greycoat Hospital School. Dorothy married Walter Williams, whose father was responsible for building a bridge across the West Dart just above where the two Darts meet. He was in the motor trade in Plymouth and bought old tram lines with which to form the bridge with planks, crosswise and wire hand rails. Dorothy's mother used the bridge to cross over to Combestone Farm to collect milk. Dorothy and Eileen live at The Bearas which was built for John Cleave, the gardener for Robert Burnard of Huccaby House. John's ancestors owned the Forest Inn when it was a thatched cottage which was burnt down.

Dorothy and Eileen are true Dartmoor stock. Talking to Dorothy recently she said that having both hips replaced had added 20 years to her life – although she was ninety earlier in the year! And to celebrate her birthday she took her great-grandchildren by Eurostar (the children had never been on a train before) to Disneyland, and for good measure renewed her driving licence as well.

The Dawes at Upper Lydgate

Above: *John 'Granfer' Dawe and Mary 'Gran' Dawe in their Sunday best, 1929.* (Eileen Exell and Dorothy Wiliams)

Left: *John Dawe with his horse.*

Top: *Ruth Dawe and George James (one of 13 children), c.1908.*

Above: *Mary and John Dawe with their granddaughter, Eileen Willcocks.*

Right: *Mary Dawe, c.1933.*
(All Eileen Exell and Dorothy Williams)

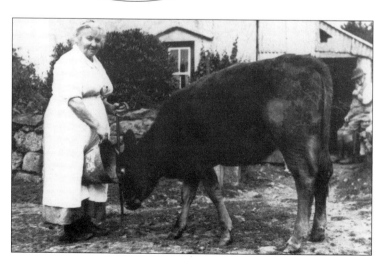

❧ Huccaby ❧

Above: *Huccaby Tor Cottage (also known as Mazedman, or Meresman, Cottage). Since the renewal of the roof the upstairs windows have been prevented from opening fully.*
(Eileen Exell and Dorothy Williams)

Above: *Dorothy James (right) and Aida Osbourne in the garden of Huccaby Tor Cottage before a Saturday night out.*

Above: *Huccaby Church, the only church in the country to be dedicated to St Raphael.*

Right: *The school desks from Postbridge School which are now used as pews in Huccaby Church.*
(Eileen Exell and Dorothy Williams)

Dartmeet Clapper Bridge from Dartmoor Illustrated, *T.A. Falcon, 1900, and (*inset*) during the 1920s.* (Hermon French and Winifred Harman)

Dartmeet from Dartmoor Illustrated, *T.A. Falcon, 1900. Today the meeting of the two rivers is very overgrown and the road surface somewhat better!*

The suspension bridge across the West Dart built by Walter Williams senr. Eileen and Dorothy used to bounce each other up and down on the flexible construction. (Eileen Exell and Dorothy Williams)

Dartmeet carpark, c.1920s. Note the open-top charabancs. (Hermon French and Winifred Harman)

Bed and
🌿 Breakfast 🌿
on Dartmoor

Top: *Frederick French with guests at Ollsbrim, teaching them how to get around the Dartmoor way.*

Above right: *More friends visiting at Ollsbrim.*

Above: *July 1951 – Mrs Bannister comes to stay at the farm.*

Right: *A postcard of 1938 of Little Meadow by Chapman & Son. It reads: 'Dear all, This is where we are staying, and we are very well looked after. Every comfort, and nice people.' The house is the same today as it was then.* (Suzanne Hutchins)

The chair in Dunnabridge Pound, 1892, with Brownberry Farmhouse in the background.
(Robert Burnard)

Dan'l Leaman of Dart-Meet-. a regular old
Moorman - a great fisherman, not innocent; so
it is said, of a little occasional poaching - Oct-9.88

Widecombe W.I., 1980s. Left to right, back: Violet Warren, ?, Miss Hamlyn, Sylvia Horton, Mrs Louie Willcocks, ?, Dawn Nosworthy, Mrs Dawe, Enid Smerdon; front: Lily Hambley, Mrs Gough, Mrs Brown, Mrs Pascoe, Miss Beard, Mrs Bamsey, ?, Ruth Parnell, ?, Mrs Easterbrook, Mrs Bell, Iris Woods.

W.I. Entertainment at a group meeting, 1980s.
1. Mabel Harrison; 2. Margaret Harris; 3. Wendy Cruze;
4. Frances Easterbrook; 5. Iris Woods; 6. Ann Murphy;
7. Barbara Guthrie; 8. Bessie Beard; 9. Gladys Mann;
10. Phyllis Pascoe; 11. Winifred French (now Harman);
12. Deborah Hannaford; 13. Violet Warren. (Phyllis Pascoe)

Chapter 10: Aspects of Community Life

❧ Women's Institute ❧

It was Freda Wilkinson who described her fellow members of Widecombe's Women's Institute as 'Wild Indians' – who on the last Thursday of each month journeyed across the moor, on foot, by car or on Beard's Bus, to their meeting in the Church House. The author's mother, Iris Woods, was a member and took her daughter-in-law Val with her whenever the meeting coincided with our visits. If there was a visiting group then entertainment was put on for the guests. There was also a monthly competition with a grand prize for the person who accrued the most points over the whole year, a competition which Iris Woods always did well in as she would be awarded points for effort even if the entry was a disaster.

Freda Wilkinson describes some of her fellow Indians:

Mrs Austin Irish of Bellever would walk alone to Huccaby, four miles each way, to a Whist drive on a winter's night over a piece of trackless moor. This was a route often used as part of a Commando toughening-up course, but her only complaint would be that she had taken longer than she reckoned because she 'didn't know the stones'.

Mrs Ned Northmore of Kingshead who was usually busy back stage wielding the teapot or washing the cups, showed her mettle in a different way during the blizzard of 1978. She and her husband were marooned in their high and lonely farmstead by half a mile of snow drifts. This was a nuisance but something they were prepared for and had experienced before. All their livestock were under cover and they had stores of food for men and beasts. The hurricane wind and weight of the snow brought the roof of one of the farm buildings down on top of all their young bullocks. Some were killed but the rest were saved when our Mrs N. (the only person small enough to do so) crawled under the collapsed roof among the panicking beasts, and forcing open an inner door, led them to safety.

Then there was Joan Steadman, the district nurse, who used to drive her own dog team over the frozen tundra to deliver Eskimo babies and to tend the sick in Labrador before she settled here at the end of her nursing career.

Gladys Mann, wife of Sylvester, has a figure that comes from a lifetime's hard work, helping her menfolk, humping hay bales, hoeing the roots, feeding and caring for lambs and children, men and cattle on the farm where her family have lived for hundreds of years.

'Mother' Brown is one of our oldest members who recently celebrated her diamond wedding with her husband Jack and a large number of their 11 children, 30 grandchildren and 44 great-grandchildren. There was no family income supplement in her day either, just hard work and thrift leavened with the sense of humour and that sturdy independence which always seem to have been characteristic of Widecombe folk.

Such people may have been isolated before the car became commonplace, but humour expressed itself in the many shows and pantomimes that were annually put on to entertain family and friends.

OFFICIAL GOLDEN JUBILEE

WIDECOMBE AND DISTRICT
WOMEN'S INSTITUTE
(21 YEARS)

1970 PROGRAMME

President ... ... Mrs. Johnson
Vice-President ... ... Mrs. Pascoe
Hon. Secretary ... ... Mrs. Daw
Hon. Treasurer ... ... Mrs. Easterbrook

Committee:
Mrs. Skinner, Mrs. Mann, Miss Beard,
Mrs. Nosworthy, Mrs. Hambley, Mrs. Warren

Monthly Meetings: Second Thursday in each month
Committee Meetings: First Thursday or as arranged by the President

---

Mrs. Northmore will be in charge of Teas.
She will co-opt members to assist her

Committee members of the Women's Institute in Widecombe at the time of the W.I. Golden Jubilee, 1970.

VE Day, 1945

Left: *John Basire with his cousins Jill and Anita raising the flag on V.E. Day, 8 May, 1945.* (John Basir)

Below: *Return of the bonfire builders. Left to right: John Basire, John French, Bernard Miners, Ted Hannaford, John Willcocks.* (Deborah Hannaford)

❧ Widecombe ❧ Amateur Dramatics

Left: *When Lily Hambley and friends were young. Mr Dunn (Uncle Tom Cobley) is in the front row with the pipe.* (Julia Morley)

Above: *Dick Whittington, 1950. Left to right, back: Herbert 'Pickles' Pascoe, ? Wilson, Dick Brown, Diana Hicks, Bernard Miners, Peter Hicks, Edna Brown, Ronald Harvey; front: Joan Miners, Ern Pascoe, Olive Miners, Frank Dowrick, Lily Hambley, Winnie Miners, Dick Brown, Joyce Miners, Mary Miners, John 'Jack' Brown (tucked behind), Kathleen Miners, Revd E.A. Newbery, Louie Palmer.* (Julia Morley)

Right: *Widecombe Wanderers, c.1953. Left to right, standing: Peter Hicks, Joyce Miners, Col Olive, Olive Kitson, Richard Brown; seated: Winnie Miners, Gwen Beard, ?, Olive Miners, Ernest Pascoe, Di Hicks, Frank Dowrick, Revd Newbery, Julia Hambley, Mary Miners, Margaret Miners (half obscured).* (Deborah Hannaford)

❧ Scouts ❦

In 1941 Henry Thorpe from Poole retired to live at Bonehill Villa and founded a scout troop. The author attended one or two meetings not long after it first started and remembers making a stool out of a plank and three nine-inch logs. Henry Thorpe died on 16 September 1948.

Above: *Left to right: Andrew Warren, Frederick Trant, Mr Henry Thorpe, David Beard.*
(William Van Straubenzee)

Right: *Left to right: John Basire, ?, Leonard Norrish, ?, Ted Hannaford. The unknown figures are thought to be Polish men in charge of a group of youngsters living in a London cellar. The scouts stayed with them in 1946.*

Below: *Left to right: Geoffrey Bamsey, Mr Henry Thorpe, David Beard (?), Anthony Beard (?), Andrew Warren (?).*
(William Van Straubenzee)

Below right: *Widecombe Scouts, 1946. Left to right: ?, Tony Brown, John Miners, Claude Warren (?), Ted Hannaford, John Basire, Leonard Norrish.*

(Deborah Hannaford)

Chapter 11: Our Distant Cousins

Genealogy has become a major area of interest over the last few years. The United States of America's bicentenary aroused in the hearts of the people the desire to know where their roots were to be found. Those seeking information in Widecombe would write to the Clerk of the Parish Council or seek help from the good offices of the Post Office, many of their letters arriving on Iris Woods' desk whereupon she would joyfully take up the challenge. The enquirers would give what information had been passed down to them – often a small detail or anecdote forming their only lead. William Armstrong Hess was one of those who wrote to the Parish Council and, at his request, Iris Woods photographed the home of his great-great-grandfather, James Cleave of Cresson Hayes at Lower Town.

The author received a letter from Mr Hess which read:

I do remember you and the wonderful pictures that you took for me. I also remember your dear mother who so graciously researched my Cleave family. I have saved her letters, and have placed your pictures in my book on Widecombe.

I initially got my desire to research the Cleave family when I found that my maternal grandmother Dora was born in Widecombe, as shown in my grandfather's Civil War records. Dora's parents first settled in Mill Creek, Ohio... [next] to what is today Cincinatti, Ohio. Their house was right on the river, and when the spring floods came they had to move everything to the second floor until the water receded. Dora's father James was a wagon builder in this country whereas he was a carpenter in England.

After grandpa Lucius came home from the Civil War he started a house-painting business. He and his brother, who lived next door, both built their houses. I hope that you are glad to have the picture of the six Cleave sisters; not all, of course, were born in England. I remember when, as a boy, the Cleave sisters would have a family party, to which my mother took me. That is how I recall the names of the sisters on the picture...

The six Cleave sisters, c.1915. (William Hess)
Left to right: Mary Grace, born 1849 in Widecombe parish, Ida, born 1862 in Ohio, USA, Sarah Ann, born 1857 in Kentucky, USA, Matilda E., born 1847 in Widecombe parish, Ledorah, born 1844 in Widecombe parish, Maud, born 1864 in Ohio, USA.

Front view of Cresson Hays as it is now. It comprises a number of old cottages and its superior stonework and style suggest that it may have been the residence of the priest of St Leonards Chapel.

Rear view of the house showing the steps to Tom Cleave's carpenter's shop.

ABBREVIATED FAMILY TREE, WITH BIRTH DATES

WILLIAM ARMSTRONG HESS JR 1942

WILLIAM ARMSTRONG HESS	1910	- JEANETTE LOWREY BLUIM	1912
AUBREY PINKERTON HESS	1885	- FLORENCE MAY WHALEY	1887
LUCIUS DANIEL WHALEY	1834	- LEDORAH CLEAVE	1844
JAMES CLEAVE	1822	- MARY IRELAND	1819
JOHN CLEAVE	1786	- CHARLOTTE	1795
WILLIAM CLEAVE	1741	- MARTHA CLEAVE	1754
WILLIAM CLEAVE	1720	- ALICE SMERDON	----

JAMES CLEAVES' FAMILY AND BRITHPLACES

1822	JAMES CLEAVE	WIDECOMBE
1819	MARY CLAEVE	WIDECOMBE
1842	JOHN M	WIDECOMBE
1844	LEDORAH (known as DORA)	WIDECOMBE
1847	MATILDA E	WIDECOMBE
1849	MARY GRACE	ENGLAND *
1852	ROBERT	ENGLAND *
1855	HENRY	ENGLAND *
1857	SARAH A	KENTUCKY
1859	MOSES	OHIO
1862	IDA	OHIO
1864	MAUD	OHIO

There is an error in the Ohio State Census between 1850 and 1860, both in ages and country of origin. As Matilda was recorded as a one-year-old in 1850 her later brothers and sisters must have been born in America.

Lucius and Ledorah Cleave Whaley, c.1900. (William Hess)

Left: *A typical request in tracing a family's roots.*

Four generations of the Caunter Nosworthy family of Canada. (Grant and Michael Nosworthy)
Left to right: Mary Caunter Nosworthy, emigrant from Widecombe in 1852
(1809-1901), George Nosworthy, son of Charles, Clarence Nosworthy, son of George (?-1982),
Charles Nosworthy, Mary's eldest son (1831-89).

John L. Webber, the local constable, who came to the village in 1862, wrote several poems about Widecombe. One, of 218 verses, contains the following:

There stands an old antique building,
Once known as Christians Hays
Where lived then the Priest, or Deacon,
Of St Leonards Church of ease.

The owner of this old building
Is the well know MR CLEAVE;
Lives in this old priestly Mansion,
What once was Christians Hays.

Cresson Hays still stands today and the Mr Cleave was John Cleave, father of James Cleave, who had already departed for America with his family.

Iris Woods was not the only person involved with those Widecombe people whose families had departed overseas. Michael Nosworthy met a Canadian Grant Nosworthy who was on a 30-day coach tour of Great Britain and managed 30 minutes in Widecombe. Knowing that his ancestors came from 'hereabouts', he enquired, fortunately, of the very person who could help him. It transpired that the family had lived at Stouts Cottages and that they had emigrated to Canada in 1852.

John Nosworthy married Anne Brinning of Buckfastleigh in 1805 and their son John Nosworthy was born in 1808 and died in 1865. He married Mary Caunter (1809-1901) and they moved to Canada in 1852. When they died they were buried in Thamsford, Ontario. Interestingly Mary's parents, George Caunter (1781-1862) and Alice Caunter (1784-1854), are commemorated on the same stone.

John and Mary had 11 children: Charles (1831-1889), Samuel (1832-1892), Henry (1834-?), Elizabeth (1837-1932), Mary Ann (1839-?), John (1841-1918), who married Margaret Montgomery (1846-1933), Eliza (1842-1904), James Caunter (1846-1936), William George (1847-?), Josiah (1849-?) and Avis (1854-?). John and Margaret had three children and Grant (1916-) married one of them, Sadie McKinnon. (They have five children and ten grandchildren.). Grant was able to tell Michael Nosworthy that John and Mary with their 11 children had all lived at Stouts Cottages and that his father had wondered how the family had squeezed into such a small place.

Thirza Nosworthy, wife of the stonemason Tom Nosworthy, wrote to me about her family tree, her grandparents being the Caunters who lived at Sweaton Farm with their 16 children. Thirza's mother Bessie married Edmund Irish of Lower Cator Farm. It would not be surprising if Thirza Nosworthy did not have distant Canadian cousins of the same name herself, given the intermingling of two old parish families.

Although the Canadian Nosworthys spell their name Norsworthy, Grant's grandfather's birth certificate spells the name Nosworthy.

Judith Hervey from Old in Australia wrote saying:

I am the family historian and visited Devon a couple of years ago where I did a lot of research in Exeter, but when I drove around my parishes of Manaton and Widecombe I was so frustrated with the usual English problem of not being able to see anything over the hedges and not being able to park anywhere to work out on a map where I was. But your book with the brilliant aerial photographs and the accompanying legends make it all so clear, and using the copies of the O.S. maps which I brought home with me I now know where I was and where I should have been.

Judith is the great-great-granddaughter of Ann Harvey (1812-88) and Thomas Payne who went to Australia in 1885. Ann Harvey was baptised on 17 November 1812 at Widecombe and looking back through the Widecombe registers Judith has all the ancient families in her 'pedigree chart', including the Caunters, Nosworthys, Leymans, Tremills, and the Frenche family which is traceable to Quintyne Crosman and Marye Man who were married on 19 January 1593.

Ann Payne (née Harvey) who was born in Widecombe and emigrated to Australia with her husband. (Judith Hervey)

LIST OF DONATIONS.

Name	£	s.	d.
His Royal Highness the Prince of Wales	20	0	0
The Dean and Chapter of Exeter	10	0	0
Mr. A. Avery			
Mr. D. J. Alliams		10	0
Mr. O. Adams		2	6
Mr. Anning		2	6
Mr. J. P. Adams		1	0
Rev. Bridgewater	1	5	0
Mr. Lionel Bulteel	2	2	0
Mrs. H. Bray		3	0
Mr. H. Bray		3	6
Mr. J. A. Bouquet		2	6
Mr. J. W. F. Bickford		2	0
Mrs. and Miss Balson		5	0
Mr. and Mrs. Bates	10	0	0
Mr. W. E. T. Bolitho		2	0
Mr. H. E. C. Braddell		2	0
Mr. J. Balsom	1	1	0
Rev. F. Bourdillon		5	0
Rev. W. P. Bastard		2	0
Mr. J. Clymo	1	1	0
Miss E. A. Carew		1	0
Mr. H. Hatt Cook		2	6
Mr. E. Cole		1	6
Rev. O. H. Cary		1	0
Rev. R. L. Collins		2	0
Mr. C.	3	0	0
Mr. E. J. Cuming	5	0	0
Dr. Cash		1	0
Mr. Irwin E. B. Cox		10	0
Mr. Drew		2	0
Mrs. T. Duguid	10	0	0
Mr. A. H. Dymond		5	0
Mr. W. Daw		5	0
Mr. R. Daw		2	0
The Misses Duguid			
Mr N. Daw		2	0
The Hon. R. Dawson	2	5	0
Mr and Mrs. W. Daw		15	0
Mr. J. Daw			
Miss M. Divett		2	0
Mr. C. Gerald Eve, F.S.I.	2	2	0
Mr. John Easterbrook, The late		1	0
Mr. John Easterbrook			
Mr. A. K Easterbrook		2	6
Mr. S. H. Easterbrook		2	6
Mr. J. H. Easterbrook, Junr.		2	6
Mr. H. Mallaby Firth	20	0	0
Mr. Sydney Firth		5	0
Mr. F. W. Firth			
Carried forward	**£136**	**5**	**6**

Name	£	s.	d.
Brought forward	**136**	**5**	**6**
Mr. G. S. Firth			
Mr. E. A. Foster	3	3	0
Miss F. Fortescue			
Mr. P. Foot	1	7	6
Mr. S. N. Fox			
Mr. J. Fleming	1	1	0
Miss Lucy Gardiner	1	1	0
Miss George		2	0
Miss Griffith		10	0
Mr. G. Hannaford		2	6
Mr. T. Hern		2	6
Mr. T. Hunt		2	0
Mr. F. Hamlyn		5	0
Mr. H. H. Hannaford, (for Bells)	5	0	0
Rev. J. Hennings		10	0
Mr. F. Hamlyn		10	0
Mr. Holding		2	0
Mrs. and Miss Hawker	2	5	6
Mrs. T. Hern		1	0
Mrs. W. Hern		10	0
Miss A. Hern		2	6
Miss N. Hern		2	6
Mr. L. Hext		2	6
Mr. G. H. Hannaford		2	6
Mr. S. Hambly		1	0
Misses F. and S. E. Harvey		2	0
Misses B. and E. J. Harvey	3	0	0
Mr. F. Horner		5	0
Mr. C. Halse		10	0
Mr. O. Harvey		2	0
Mrs. Alers Hankey	10	0	0
Miss Hook		5	0
Mr. E. Irish		2	0
Mr. T. k. Irish		2	0
Mrs. Lloyd Jones		1	0
Miss Jordan		2	0
The Late Sir Penrose G. Julyan		10	0
Mr. Walter Kennaway, C.M.G.		10	0
Mr. William Kennaway		5	0
Mr. and Mrs. John Kitson	15	0	0
Mr. and Mrs. King		2	0
Mr. R. Kernick		1	0
Mrs. M. L. Kennaway		2	6
Mrs. Levett		2	6
Mr. A. C. Loveys		2	6
Mr. H. Langridge Lane		2	6
Miss Morice	20	0	0
Miss F. Morris		5	0
Capt. E.F. Morrison-Bell, M.P.			
Carried forward	**£228**	**14**	**0**

Name	£	s.	d.
Brought forward	**228**	**14**	
Mr. J. Mann	1	0	0
Mr. W. Mann			
Mr. Oliver Mann	1	0	0
Miss A. Morris			
Mr. Norman Mackinlay	2	2	0
Mrs. M. Mackinlay	2	2	0
Misses Mackinlay	1	1	0
Mr. W. H. Mortimer	1	1	0
Mr. F. Mears		5	0
Miss C. Morrison	1	0	0
Miss Moore			
Mr. T. Mann		1	0
Mr. G. Nosworthy			
Mr. F. Nosworthy		1	0
Mr. R. Nosworthy		1	0
Miss T. Nosworthy		10	0
Mr. Ambrose Nosworthy		2	6
Mr. W. Nosworthy		2	6
Mr. J. Nosworthy		2	0
Mrs. W. Nosworthy		2	6
Mr. A. Norrish		10	0
Rev. John T. Pickering	5	0	0
Misses Phillips	2	2	0
Rev. Poulden			
Mr. A. L. Poulter	5	0	0
Mr. J. L. Prowse		2	6
Parishioners		5	0
Rev. W. A. Prideaux	1	1	0
Mr. T. Roberts	2	2	0
Mr. Lancaster Rose	2	2	0
Mrs. C. Robinson	2	2	0
Lord Revelstoke	10	0	0
Mr. E. Roberts			
Mr. A. N. Radcliffe	20	0	0
Mr. D. Radcliffe	1	1	0
Mrs. Radcliffe		2	6
Miss Radcliffe	2	10	0
Miss R. Radcliffe	2	10	0
Miss M. Radcliffe		10	0
Master W. Radcliffe		5	0
Miss Rose			
Hon. W. F. D. Smith, M.P.	15	0	0
Mr. F. P. T. Struben	5	5	0
Miss Sanders	1	1	0
Messrs. Sawdye and Son		10	0
Mrs. Stone	2	2	0
Mrs. H. Sharland	2	10	0
Mr. H. Soper		5	0
Mr. W. M. G. Singer	20	0	0
Mr. J. S Scrimgeour	20	0	0
Miss C. Scrimgeour		1	3
Carried forward	**£359**	**5**	**6**

Name	£	s.	d.
Brought forward	**359**	**5**	**6**
Mrs. Scrimgeour	2	2	0
Miss Skinner (the late)	1	0	0
Sir Spencer Stanhope, K.C.B.	5	5	0
Rev. R. Scrimgeour	2	2	0
Miss A. E. Thomson	1	1	0
Miss E. Tucker		10	0
Mr. T. Townsend			
Major B. C. Tucker	1	1	0
Mrs. Wycliffe Taylor	20	0	0
Mr. A. Thomson	1	1	0
Miss E. Tucker	2	2	0
Mr. H. W. Thomson	2	2	6
Mr. G. Vanstone		2	0
Mr. R. Vicary		1	0
Mr. W. Vicary	1	1	0
The Misses Whidborne	1	0	6
Rev. A. A. Woollcombe	1	0	0
Colonel E. S. Walcott, C.B.		10	6
Mr. J. Wills		10	6
Mr. W. Wellington	1	2	6
Mr. W. Whiteway		2	6
Mr. A. Warren	4	0	0
Mr. C. W. Wills	10	0	0
Mr. N. B. Williams	5	5	0
Mr. Wilson			
Mr. H. Wenham	20	0	0
Rev. F. Young	24	15	6
Visitors Offering, Widecombe Church	10	4	6
Harvest Festival	3	16	6
Per Rev. John T. Pickering	1	18	0
Proceeds of Concert at Widecombe	8	9	8
Interest, Lloyds Bank			
	£478	**19**	**8**

THE CATHEDRAL OF THE MOOR

The vicar, churchwardens and parishioners have always faced mounting costs for repairs to the 'Cathedral of the Moor' and, although it must have often been tempting to put such repairs off until the following year, the nettle has always been grasped. The present vicar and churchwardens face another huge challenge and have launched, as part of the fundraising, an interesting scheme called 'A Life Remembered'; a book of remembrance where names of loved ones can be entered for a small fee.

The pamphlet which describes this scheme states:

St Pancras Church, Widecombe-in-the-Moor, is far more than a small place of worship for our local community. Each year many thousands of people come from all over the world to see Dartmoor, visit the village and make a beeline for the church. Our local congregation is very small, but our many visitors tell us how much St Pancras means to them when they visit year round, welcoming the prayerful environment of an ancient place of Christian worship.

At the beginning of the 21st century, Widecombe is facing major repairs to the tower, which needs repointing, and to the floor of the ringing chamber and the bell frame, which need replacing. This is a major undertaking for the small community which will have to meet a huge repair bill.

We rely on the generosity of people with a love of the church to help meet the £100 000 required to ensure that the Cathedral of the Moor will stand to serve future generations.

Robert Dymond of Blackslade worked very hard in the late 1800s to raise monies for repairs to the roof of the church and for that purpose he wrote and edited the first book to be written about Widecombe-in-the-Moor, *Things Old and New*, to be followed by *Newspaper*, the sales from both of which helped to finance the repairs. (It was in the latter publication that Dymond recorded that there were those alive in the parish who remembered the ruins of the drawbridge to North Hall.).

In 1905/6 the vicar, John T. Pickering, ably assisted by H. Mallaby Firth and J. S. Scrimgeour, were in the thick of the repairs and the report on and subscription list (*left*) make very interesting reading, especially in comparison with the problems encountered today, for they set out to raise the sum of £476.0s.1d. to cover repairs to the tower almost identical to those required nearly a century later. The final paragraph of the report reads:

We cannot conclude without a reminder that although much has been done, still much remains to put this 'Cathedral of the Moor' in such proper order as befits the House of God, and which it is desirable should be attended to whenever the needful funds can be raised for the purpose.

Widecombe Bellringers. (Deborah Hannaford) *Left to right, back: Geoff Hannaford, Reg Norrish, Les Edworthy, Ern Pascoe, Frank Dowrick; front: Mrs Newbery (vicar's wife), Bill Miners, Lady Sayer, Revd Newbery.*

SUBSCRIBERS

John A. Baker, Exeter, Devon
Mrs D. Basire, Lezant, Cornwall
Dr & Mrs John Batterham, Poundsgate, Devon
Dorothy R. Baty, Liverton, Newton Abbot, Devon
Anthony E. Beard, Widecombe-in-the-Moor,
    Devon
Stephen J. Beard, Widecombe-in-the-Moor, Devon
Trevor P. Beard, Widecombe-in-the-Moor, Devon
Caroline F. Belam, Ludgate, West Buckfastleigh,
    Devon
Revd John & Dr Hazel Bell, Kingsnympton, Devon
E. Phyllis Bell, Widecombe, Devon
Reg & Betty Bellamy, Postbridge, Devon/York
Mr J. D. & Mrs C. J. Bewsher, Paignton, Devon
C. H. Bolton, Kilmington, Axminster, Devon
Simon & Annabel Booty, Poundsgate, Devon
A. & S. Boult, Widecombe-in-the-Moor, Devon
Kath Brewer, Torquay, Devon
Dave Brewer, Meopham, Kent
Mrs D. Brickl, Postbridge, Yelverton, Devon
Brixington Junior School, Exmouth, Devon
Mr A. R. Brown, Kingsteignton, Newton Abbot,
    Devon
Mr Ashel Richard Brown, Sudbury, Suffolk
K. J. Burrow, Bucks Cross, Bideford, Devon
Kristian Carter, Warminster, Wiltshire
Michael H. Churchward, Widecombe-in-the-
    Moor, Devon
Ann & Roger Claxton, Widecombe-in-the-Moor,
    Devon
Mr & Mrs W. Coaker, Widecombe-in-the-Moor,
    Devon
R. C. Cornish, Liverton, Newton Abbot, Devon
Ronnie & Marian Constant, Widecombe-in-the-
    Moor, Devon
Ann Darlington, Merriott, Somerset
Dartmoor National Park Authority, Bovey Tracey,
    Devon
Gary & Sheenagh Denham, Widecombe-in-the-
    Moor, Devon
Terry Dowrick, Exmouth, Devon
Mr & Mrs P. W. Dracup, Broadford, Widecombe-in-
    the-Moor, Devon
Audrey G. Fairbrother, Poundsgate, Newton
    Abbot, Devon
Richard, Rosalind & Oliver Field, Plymouth,
    Devon
Lynne & Michael Fillery, Maidstone, Kent
Mrs M. Foggin, New South Wales, Australia
Mr & Mrs W. Foster, Tavistock, Devon
Bessie A. French, Ponsworthy, Devon
Bridget Fursdon, Liverton, Devon
Ann Garfield (née Nosworthy), Peterborough
Mr & Mrs G. W. Gilliam, Ringmore, Kingsbridge,
    Devon
Jean V. Gooch,
142

Dr T. & Mrs E. Greeves, Tavistock, Devon
Paul & Freda Griffiths, Cronton, Cheshire
Mr & Mrs D. Grigg, Plymouth, Devon
Stella Grimsey, Overton, Hants
Gavin Grimsey, Bovey Tracey, Devon
Mrs R. Griver, Louth, Lincs.
Mr P. Hamilton Leggatt BSc, Tavistock, Devon
C. & W. Harman, Truro, Cornwall
Bruce & Diana Harris, Ipplepen, Devon
Mr & Mrs Harris, Okehampton, Devon
Judith Hervey, Brisbane, Australia
Maurice H. Hill, Ilfracombe, Devon
Mrs Stella Hooton (née Brown), Harrold,
    Bedfordshire
Brian & Suzanne Hutchins, Little Meadow,
    Widecombe-in-the-Moor, Devon
Mr & Mrs Mark Hutchins, Widecombe-in-the-
    Moor, Devon
Roy V. M. Jeffery, Broadclyst, Exeter, Devon
J. Loveys Jervoise, Sampford Courtenay, Devon
Colin C. Kilvington, Stoke, Plymouth, Devon
N. Lamb, Widecombe-in-the-Moor, Devon
Brian Le Messurier, Exeter, Devon
David Chown Lee, Exmouth, Devon
Miss J. Lee, Tavistock, Devon
Betty S. Legg, Portchester, Hants.
J. A. Lieurance, Poundsgate, Newton Abbot, Devon
Douglas Marsh, Chagford, Devon
Christopher Mayhead, Widecombe-in-the-Moor,
    Devon
Brian Mead, Fardel, Cornwood, Devon
Edward Miners, Widecombe-in-the-Moor, Devon
Andy N. Mitchell, Westerham, Kent
T. Monckton, Portchester, Hants.
Mr B. Monckton, Lincoln
Julia & Cliff Morley, Newton Abbot, Devon
Rodney & Jean Mortimore, Ashburton, Devon
Lloyd & Rosemary Mortimore, Widecombe-in-the-
    Moor, Devon
Arch & Audrey Mortimore, Widecombe-in-the-
    Moor, Devon
Victoria Mary Naylor, Plymstock, Devon
S. C. Needham, Widecombe-in-the-Moor, Devon
David & Mary Neilson, Portchester, Fareham,
    Hants.
Roderick & Elizabeth Newbolt-Young, Chittleford
    Farm, Widecombe-in-the-Moor
Steve Newell, Flackwell Heath, Bucks.
M.S. & R. Norrish, Widecombe-in-the-Moor,
    Devon
Robert A. Nosworthy, Harrisburg, PA, USA
Stephen G. Nosworthy, Exmouth, Devon
Eileen & Michael Nosworthy, Widecombe-in-the-
    Moor, Devon
Mrs Karen R. O'Flaherty (née Woods), Reigate,
    Surrey
Sheena Odle, Tavistock, Devon
J. & M. Olszewski, Penzance, Cornwall
Mr N. J. Osborne, Westbury, Wiltshire
Mr & Mrs K. Owen, Tavistock, Devon

Mike & Jenny Pascoe, Widecombe-in-the-Moor, Devon

Mrs Phyllis Pascoe, Widecombe-in-the-Moor, Devon

Mike & Jane Passmore, Exeter, Devon

Andrew Passmore, Exeter, Devon

Mr L. E. Pavitt, Crewkerne, Somerset

S. L. Peach, Widecombe-in-the-Moor, Devon

Mrs Hazel Pearse, North Bovey, Newton Abbot, Devon

Marion Pelham, London N10

Mr & Mrs R. M. Perry, Plymouth, Devon

Terry & Margaret Phipps, Poundsgate, Newton Abbot, Devon

H. G. Price (former Parish Clerk), Widecombe-in-the-Moor, Devon

Audrey Prizeman, Plymouth, Devon

R. John K. Prouse, Brecon, Powys

Mr & Mrs D. W. Puttick, Eastbourne, Sussex

June M. Puttick, Eastbourne, Sussex

Ken Rickard, Lydford, Devon

Mary Rivers-Moore, South Brent, Devon

D. G. M. Roberts, Hassocks, Sussex

Mr & Mrs Rolfe, Tamerton Foliot, Plymouth, Devon

Mr & Mrs Rolfe, Lower Dimson, Devon

L. W. Rowe, Newton Abbot, Devon

Mrs Jenny Sanders, Tavistock, Devon

Elizabeth Saunders, Newton Abbot, Devon

Christopher G. W. Simmons, Hayes, Bromley, Kent

Mary Slade, Ponsworthy, Newton Abbot, Devon

John E. Smith, Turnchapel, Plymouth, Devon

Robert Somerville, Michelcombe, Holne, Devon

Robert Steemson, Postbridge, Devon

Sir William Van Straubenzee,

Peggy Strowger, Cosham

J. J. Taylor, Dorchester, Dorset

Mary Tester, Poundsgate, Newton Abbot, Devon

Mrs P. Theobald (née German), Haslemere, Surrey

Nel Tullis, Ashburton/Kenton, Devon

Mr Andrew Valli, Sydney, Australia

Mrs C. Valli (née Hall), Chipperfield, Kings Langley, Herts.

Mrs N. K. Van Der Kiste, South Brent, Devon

John Vickery, Poundsgate, Newton Abbot, Devon

Mrs S. Walcot, Ponsworthy, Devon

Mr. G. Waldron, Plymouth, Devon

Mrs B. B. J. Wale, Kingskerswell, Newton Abbot, Devon

John F. W. Walling, Newton Abbot, Devon

Roy Ward, "Ward End", Brixham, Devon

A. Watson, Exeter, Devon

Mr J. Weymouth, South Brent, Devon

Geoffrey Weymouth, Ponsworthy, Newton Abbot, Devon

B. & P. Whale, Widecombe-in-the-Moor, Devon

Claud & Alison Whale, Widecombe-in-the-Moor, Devon

Alan Wheelhouse, Ilsington, Newton Abbot, Devon

Freda Wilkinson, Poundsgate, Newton Abbot, Devon

Dorothy Williams, Hexworthy, Yelverton, Devon

Graham Wooding, Lower Cator, Widecombe-in-the-Moor, Devon

Andrew, Janet, Anna & Luke Woods, Portchester, Hants.

Rob, Margy, Christina & Jonathan Woods, Didcot, Oxon

The Revd & Mrs Geoffrey Wrayford, Minehead, Somerset

Mrs P. J. Wuchatsch, Victoria, Australia

Revd Leonard James McCrea, the author's grandfather who lived at Dunstone Cottage.

Also available in the Community History Series:
The Book of Bampton Caroline Seward
Clearbrook, The Story of a Dartmoor Hamlet Pauline Hemery
The Book of Cornwood and Lutton, Photographs and Reminiscences compiled by the People of the Parish
The Ellacombe Book Sydney R. Langmead
The Book of Grampound with Creed Amy Bane and Mary Oliver
The Book of Lamerton Ann Cole and Friends
Lanner – A Cornish Mining Parish Sharron Schwartz and Roger Parker
The Book of Manaton Compiled by the people of the parish
The Book of Meavy Pauline Hemery
The Book of Morchard Bishop Jeff Kingaby
The Book of North Newton J.C. Robins and K.C. Robins
The Book of Plymtree, The Parish and Its People compiled and edited by Tony Eames
The Book of Porlock Dennis Corner
Postbridge – The Heart of Dartmoor Reg Bellamy
The Book of Stithians, The Changing Face of a Cornish Parish Stithians Parish History Group
The Book of Torbay, A Century of Celebration Frank Pearce
The Book of Trusham Alick Cameron
Widecombe–in–the–Moor Stephen Woods
Woodbury, The Twentieth Century Revisited compiled by Roger Stokes

Forthcoming titles in the Community History Series:
The Book of Chittlehampton Various
The Book of Bickington Stuart Hands
The Book of Bickleigh Various
The Book of Brixham Frank Pearce
The Book of Helston Derek Carter
The Book of High Bickington Avril Stone
The Book of Ilsington Dick Wills
The Book of Luppitt Various
The Lustleigh Book Various
The Book of Mabe Bryant and Bryant
The Book of Meneage Derek Carter
The Book of the Scilly Isles Various
The Book of Severne Various
The Book of Silverton Graham Parnell
The Book of South Tawton and South Zeal Roy and Ursula Radford

Further information:
If you would like to order a book or find out more about having your parish featured in this series, please contact The Editor, Community History Series, Halsgrove House, Lower Moor Way, Tiverton Business Park, Tiverton, Devon, EX16 6SS, tel: 01884 243242/e-mail:sales@halsgrove.com
If you are interested in a particular photograph in this volume, it may be possible to supply you with a copy of the image.